The Isms: Modern Doctrines and Movements

Nationalism

Opposing Viewpoints

REVISED EDITION

Other Volumes Available in the *ISMS SERIES:*

# Nationalism

## Opposing Viewpoints

REVISED EDITION

Bruno Leone

Greenhaven Press
577 Shoreview Park Road
St. Paul, Minnesota 55126

Library of Congress Cataloging-in-Publication Data

Nationalism : opposing viewpoints
  (The Isms)
  Includes bibliographies and index.
  1. Nationalism—Addresses, essays, lectures.
I. Leone, Bruno, 1939-          II. Series.
JC311.N325   1986          320.5'4          86-324
ISBN 0-89908-362-5 (pbk.)
ISBN 0-89908-387-0 (lib. bdg.)

Second Edition
Revised

"Congress shall make no law . . .
abridging the freedom of speech,
or of the press."

first amendment to the U.S. Constitution

The basic foundation of our democracy is the first amendment
guarantee of freedom of expression. The Opposing Viewpoints
books are dedicated to the concept of this basic freedom and the
idea that it is more important to practice it than to enshrine it.

# Contents

# Chapter 3: Nationalism and Revolution

# Chapter 4: Contemporary Nationalism in the Middle East

# Why Consider Opposing Viewpoints?

*"It is better to debate a question without settling it than to settle a question without debating it."*

Joseph Joubert (1754-1824)

### The Importance of Examining Opposing Viewpoints

The purpose of the Opposing Viewpoints books, and this book in particular, is to present balanced, and often difficult to find, opposing points of view on complex and sensitive issues.

Probably the best way to become informed is to analyze the positions of those who are regarded as experts and well studied on issues. It is important to consider every variety of opinion in an attempt to determine the truth. Opinions from the mainstream of society should be examined. But also important are opinions that are considered radical, reactionary, or minority as well as those stigmatized by some other uncomplimentary label. An important lesson of history is the eventual acceptance of many unpopular and even despised opinions. The ideas of Socrates, Jesus, and Galileo are good examples of this.

Readers will approach this book with their own opinions on the issues debated within it. However, to have a good grasp of one's own viewpoint, it is necessary to understand the arguments of those with whom one disagrees. It can be said that those who do not completely understand their adversary's point of view do not fully understand their own.

A persuasive case for considering opposing viewpoints has been presented by John Stuart Mill in his work *On Liberty*. When examining controversial issues it may be helpful to reflect on this suggestion:

> The only way in which a human being can make some approach to knowing the whole of a subject, is by hearing what can be said about it by persons of every variety of opinion, and studying all modes in which it can be looked at by every character of mind. No wise man ever acquired his wisdom in any mode but this.

## Analyzing Sources of Information

The Opposing Viewpoints books include diverse materials taken from magazines, journals, books, and newspapers, as well as statements and position papers from a wide range of individuals, organizations and governments. This broad spectrum of sources helps to develop patterns of thinking which are open to the consideration of a variety of opinions.

## Pitfalls to Avoid

A pitfall to avoid in considering opposing points of view is that of regarding one's own opinion as being common sense and the most rational stance and the point of view of others as being only opinion and naturally wrong. It may be that another's opinion is correct and one's own is in error.

Another pitfall to avoid is that of closing one's mind to the opinions of those with whom one disagrees. The best way to approach a dialogue is to make one's primary purpose that of understanding the mind and arguments of the other person and not that of enlightening him or her with one's own solutions. More can be learned by listening than speaking.

It is my hope that after reading this book the reader will have a deeper understanding of the issues debated and will appreciate the complexity of even seemingly simple issues on which good and honest people disagree. This awareness is particularly important in a democratic society such as ours where people enter into public debate to determine the common good. Those with whom one disagrees should not necessarily be regarded as enemies, but perhaps simply as people who suggest different paths to a common goal.

## Developing Basic Reading and Thinking Skills

In this book carefully edited opposing viewpoints are purposely placed back to back to create a running debate; each viewpoint is preceded by a short quotation that best expresses the author's main argument. This format instantly plunges the reader into the midst of a controversial issue and greatly aids that reader in mastering the basic skill of recognizing an author's point of view.

A number of basic skills for critical thinking are practiced in the activities that appear throughout the books in the series. Some of the skills are:

*Evaluating Sources of Information* The ability to choose from among alternative sources the most reliable and accurate source in relation to a given subject.

*Separating Fact from Opinion* The ability to make the basic distinction between factual statements (those that can be demonstrated or verified empirically) and statements of opinion (those that are beliefs or attitudes that cannot be proved).

*Identifying Stereotypes* The ability to identify oversimplified, exaggerated descriptions (favorable or unfavorable) about people and insulting statements about racial, religious or national groups, based upon misinformation or lack of information.

*Recognizing Ethnocentrism* The ability to recognize attitudes or opinions that express the view that one's own race, culture, or group is inherently superior, or those attitudes that judge another culture or group in terms of one's own.

It is important to consider opposing viewpoints and equally important to be able to critically analyze those viewpoints. The activities in this book are designed to help the reader master these thinking skills. Statements are taken from the book's viewpoints and the reader is asked to analyze them. This technique aids the reader in developing skills that not only can be applied to the viewpoints in this book, but also to situations where opinionated spokespersons comment on controversial issues. Although the activities are helpful to the solitary reader, they are most useful when the reader can benefit from the interaction of group discussion.

Using this book and others in the series should help readers develop basic reading and thinking skills. These skills should improve the readers' ability to understand what they read. Readers should be better able to separate fact from opinion, substance from rhetoric and become better consumers of information in our media-centered culture.

This volume of the Opposing Viewpoints books does not advocate a particular point of view. Quite the contrary! The very nature of the book leaves it to the reader to formulate the opinions he or she finds most suitable. My purpose as publisher is to see that this is made possible by offering a wide range of viewpoints which are fairly presented.

David L. Bender
Publisher

11

# Preface to
# First Edition

In his compelling essay, "The Duties of Man," the nineteenth-century Italian patriot Giuseppe Mazzini wrote:

> O my Brothers! Love your country. Our country is our home, the home which God has given us, placing therein a numerous family which we love and are loved by, and with which we have a more intimate and quicker communion of feeling and thought than with others; a family which by its concentration upon a given spot, and by the homogeneous nature of its elements, is destined for a special kind of activity.

Emotional and farseeing, Mazzini's sentiments were expressive of nationalism, a principal force shaping nineteenth-century European and twentieth-century world civilization.

Modern nationalism began as a liberal reaction to the autocracy of the dynastic states of Europe. Before the nineteenth century, nationality was based upon personal allegiance to a monarch. Thus a Frenchman living in 1785 would rightfully consider himself a subject of the Bourbon King Louis XVI rather than a citizen of France. Moreover, the Frenchman need not even have been French by language and tradition as most of the dynastic states were made up of a mixture (often hostile to each other) of culturally diverse people.

During the first half of the nineteenth century, however, the idea of allegiance to a geographical nation (not an individual) composed of people joined by language, custom, and a common historical tradition proved too seductive to resist. Inspired by nationalistic writers like Jean Paul Marat in France, Giuseppe Mazzini in Italy and Johann Wolfgang von Goethe in Germany, one by one the states of Europe underwent a change which was more than cosmetic as governments and national boundaries were reforged along the logical lines of cultural distinctiveness. In France, Louis XVI was dethroned, eventually beheaded, and the monarch replaced by a Republican form of government. Germany, which at one time was composed of over three hundred independent principalities, was moving toward unification under the leadership of Prussia, the most powerful of the independent German states. Italy was following a path similar to Germany as Italian nationalists sought to reunite their homeland and rid it of foreign rule. And the Balkan states of Europe aspired to free themselves from the domination of the Ottoman Turks, a domination which had lasted over three hundred years.

Moreover, unification and freedom from foreign and dynastic rule were not the sole or primary aims of early nationalism. The far more blessed goal of a free constitution under which individual rights supplanted governmental despotism was considered of even greater consequence. In fact, the promise of personal liberty and the general advancement of the material well-being of an enlightened citizenry were the motivating factors underlying the nationalistic movements of the first half of the nineteenth-century.

Finally, the lofty prospects of peace, cooperation and brotherhood among the free and newly emergent states of Europe were added adornments. The relationship of peoples both within and between states would be governed by humanitarian principles. Indeed, a liberal cocoon appeared to be enveloping the map and temperament of Europe.

But by the middle of the century, the character of nationalism experienced a fundamental change. As the cocoon broke open, in lieu of the promised harmony, the monster of chauvinism showed its ugly head. Humanitarianism was replaced by aggression, the exhaltation of the individual by the exhaltation of the state. Whereas the state at first was considered the means to achieve a cherished end, the state now became an end in itself, an organic unity which enjoyed an existence exclusive of those residing within its borders.

And another powerful and more ominous feature of this "new" nationalism was its expansionist tendency. The old nationalism aspired to unify the nation—one nation in one state and little else. The new nationalism sanctioned the imposition of one nation's values and standards upon another. All was fair game in the arena of international politics, territorial expansion included. The imperialistic totalitarian movements of the twentieth century were the logical termination of this aggressive brand of nationalism.

Since its impact first was felt in nineteenth-century Europe, nationalism has been an irrepressible movement which has left (and continues to leave) its peculiar imprint upon the course of history. Yet as a shaping force in world civilization, nationalism can be either beneficial or destructive. When governments advocate international assistance, tolerance and fellowship without necessarily sacrificing the national distinctiveness with which a people may identify and grow, nationalism can be a constructive force. Conversely, when exclusivism is preached and imperialism practiced, nationalism can be the most divisive and potentially the most catastrophic force in the history of humankind.

# Preface to Second Edition

It is with pleasure and an enormous degree of satisfaction that the second edition of Greenhaven Press's *ISMS Series: Opposing Viewpoints* has been published. The Series was so well received when it initially was made available in 1978 that plans for its revision were almost immediately formulated. During the following years, the enthusiasm of librarians and classroom teachers provided the editor with the necessary encouragement to complete the project.

While the Opposing Viewpoints format of the series has remained the same, each of the books has undergone a major revision. Because the series is developed along historical lines, materials were added or deleted in the opening chapters only where historical interpretations have changed or new sources were uncovered. The final chapters of each book have been comprehensively recast to reflect changes in the national and international situations since the original titles were published.

The Series began with six titles: *Capitalism, Communism, Internationalism, Nationalism, Racism,* and *Socialism.* A new and long overdue title, *Feminism,* has been added and several additional ones are being considered for the future. The editor offers his deepest gratitude to the dedicated and talented editorial staff of Greenhaven Press for its countless and invaluable contributions. A special thanks goes to Bonnie Szumski, whose gentle encouragement and indomitable aplomb helped carry the developing manuscripts over many inevitable obstacles. Finally, the editor thanks all future readers and hopes that the 1986 edition of the *ISMS Series* will enjoy the same reception as its predecessor.

# Nineteenth-Century Nationalism: ''The Old and the New''

# Introduction

Perhaps no nineteenth-century thinkers better typify the contrast between the "old" and the "new" nationalism than Giuseppe Mazzini and Heinrich von Treitschke. Although both were ardent nationalists, the similarities ended there. Mazzini was a high principled moralist who advocated harmony and cooperation between nations; von Treitschke was an amoral Machiavellian who condoned self-serving militarism. Mazzini regarded offensive warfare as a sin against God and man; von Treitschke viewed all warfare as a "sacred" rite of purification in which "the chaff is winnowed from the wheat." Mazzini preached that the state derived its just powers from the people; von Treitschke held the reverse to be true. As the following viewpoints will illustrate, even the tone and style of their works highlighted their differences. Mazzini is passionate, emotional and high-sounding, while von Treitschke always remains controlled, detached and direct.

The viewpoints by Gladstone and Rohrbach are also illustrative of the "old" versus the "new" nationalism. A prophet of nineteenth-century liberalism, Gladstone was convinced that the advancement of European civilization would be realized only if the spirit of fellowship existed among peoples and states. Conversely, the jingoistic Rohrbach believed that the mission and destiny of Germany should take precedent over such visionary fancies as a fellowship of European nations.

*"If you do not embrace the whole human family in your love, if you do not confess your faith in its unity...you disobey your law of life."*

# Nationalism: The Exaltation of the Individual

Giuseppe Mazzini

Giuseppe Mazzini (1805-1872) was the founder of *Giovine Italia* (young Italy), a movement which advocated the independence and unification of Italy under a Republican form of government. A humanitarian and internationalist, he also founded *Giovine Europa* (young Europe) in hopes of joining all Europe into a union of free peoples. Mazzini was a persevering and dauntless patriot who was sentenced to death three times for participating in revolutions aimed at unifying Italy.

As you read, consider the following questions:

1. What does Mazzini say are one's duties to humanity?
2. What does he believe is the purpose of the nation?

From *The Duties of Man, and Other Essays* by Giuseppe Mazzini. An Everyman's Library Edition. Published in the United States by E.P. Dutton, and reprinted with their permission.

Your first Duties—first, at least, in importance—are...to Humanity. You are *men* before you are *citizens* or *fathers*. If you do not embrace the whole human family in your love, if you do not confess your faith in its unity—consequent on the unity of God—and in the brotherhood of the Peoples who are appointed to reduce that unity to fact—if wherever one of your fellowmen groans, wherever the dignity of human nature is violated by falsehood or tyranny, you are not prompt, being able, to succour that wretched one, or do not feel yourself called, being able, to fight for the purpose of relieving the deceived or oppressed—you disobey your law of life, or do not comprehend the religion which will bless the future.

## Disappearance of Bad Governments

But what can *each* of you, with his isolated powers, *do* for the moral improvement, for the progress of Humanity...? God gave you this means when he gave you a Country, when, like a wise overseer of labour, who distributes the different parts of the work according to the capacity of the workmen, he divided Humanity into distinct groups upon the face of our globe, and thus planted the seeds of nations. Bad governments have disfigured the design of God, which you may see clearly marked out, as far, at least, as regards Europe, by the courses of the great rivers, by the lines of the lofty mountains, and by other geographical conditions; they have disfigured it by conquest, by greed, by jealousy of the just sovereignty of others; disfigured it so much that to-day there is perhaps no nation except England and France whose confines correspond to this design. They did not, and they do not, recognise any country except their own families and dynasties, the egoism of caste. But the divine design will infallibly be fulfilled. Natural divisions, the innate spontaneous tendencies of the peoples, will replace the arbitrary divisions sanctioned by bad governments. The map of Europe will be remade. The Countries of the People will rise, defined by the voice of the free, upon the ruins of the Countries of Kings and privileged castes. Between these Countries there will be harmony and brotherhood. And then the work of Humanity for the general amelioration, for the discovery and application of the real law of life, carried on in association and distributed according to local capacities, will be accomplished by peaceful and progressive development; then each of you, strong in the affections and in the aid of many millions of men speaking the same language, endowed with the same tendencies, and educated by the same historic tradition, may hope by your personal effort to benefit the whole of Humanity....

## Purpose of the Nation

[Italy] is our home, the home which God has given us, placing therein a numerous family which we love and are loved by, and with which we have a more intimate and quicker communion of feeling and thought than with others; a family which by its concentration upon a given spot, and by the homogeneous nature of its elements, is destined for a special kind of activity. Our Country is our field of labour; the products of our activity must go forth from it for the benefit of the whole earth; but the instruments of labour which we can use best and most effectively exist in it, and we may not reject them without being unfaithful to God's purpose and diminishing our own strength. In labouring according to true principles for our Country we are labouring for Humanity; our Country is the fulcrum of the lever which we have to wield for the common good. If we give up this fulcrum we run the risk of becoming useless to our Country and to Humanity. Before *associating* ourselves with the Nations which compose Humanity we must exist as a Nation. There can be no association except among equals; and you have no recognized collective existence.

**Italy Before Unification**

Humanity is a great army moving to the conquest of unknown lands, against powerful and wary enemies. The Peoples are the different corps and divisions of that army. Each has a post entrusted to it; each a special operation to perform; and the common victory depends on the exactness with which the different operations are carried out. Do not disturb the order of the battle. Do not abandon the banner which God has given you. Wherever you may be, into the midst of whatever people circumstances may have driven you, fight for the liberty of that people if the moment calls for it; but fight as Italians, so that the blood which you shed may win honour and love, not for you only, but for your Country. And may the constant thought of your soul be for Italy, may all the acts of your life be worthy of her, and may the standard beneath which you range yourselves to work for Humanity be Italy's. Do not say *I;* say *we.* Be every one of you an incarnation of your Country, and feel himself and make himself responsible for his fellow-countrymen; let each one of you learn to act in such a way that in him men shall respect and love his Country.

*"If [the state] neglects its strength in order
to promote the idealistic aspirations of man,
it repudiates its own nature and perishes."*

# Nationalism: The Exaltation of the State

Heinrich von Treitschke

A professor of history at the University of Berlin, Heinrich von Treitschke (1834-1896) was one of Germany's most articulate and fervent nationalists. He envisioned the state as an organic entity to whose will the citizenry should respond with a slavish obedience. Without the state, citizens lose their reason for being. He believed that the German nation of his day was on the threshold of a glorious political hegemony and he demanded the myopic loyalty of its people. The nationalistic, anti-Semitic, and antiliberal bias that distinguish his works, clearly earmark von Treitschke as an intellectual forerunner of twentieth-century Nazism.

As you read, consider the following questions:

1. How does von Treitschke define the power of the state?
2. What services does he believe the state provides?
3. Why is war essential for a nation, according to the author?

Heinrich von Treitschke, *Politics, Volume I*, New York: Macmillan, 1916.

The rational task of a legally constituted people, conscious of a destiny, is to assert its rank in the world's hierarchy and in its measure to participate in the great civilizing mission of mankind.

Further, if we examine our definition of the State as "the people legally united as an independent entity," we find that it can be more briefly put thus: "The State is the public force for Offence and Defence...." [It] protects and embraces the people's life, regulating its external aspects on every side. It does not ask primarily for opinion, but demands obedience, and its laws must be obeyed, whether willingly or no....

The State is not an Academy of Arts. If it neglects its strength in order to promote the idealistic aspirations of man, it repudiates its own nature and perishes. This is in truth for the State equivalent to the sin against the Holy Ghost, for it is indeed a mortal error in the State to subordinate itself for sentimental reasons to a foreign Power, as we Germans have often done to England....

We have described the State as an independent force. This pregnant theory of independence implies firstly so absolute a moral supremacy that the State cannot legitimately tolerate any power above its own, and secondly a temporal freedom entailing a variety of material resources adequate to its protection against hostile influences. Legal sovereignty, the State's complete independence of any other earthly power, is so rooted in its nature that it may be said to be its very standard and criterion....

## War Is Essential for the State

It is clear that the international agreements which limit the power of a State are not absolute, but voluntary self-restrictions. Hence, it follows that the establishment of a permanent international Arbitration Court is incompatible with the nature of the State, which could at all events only accept the decision of such a tribunal in cases of second- or third-rate importance. When a nation's existence is at stake there is no outside Power whose impartiality can be trusted....It is, moreover, a point of honour for a State to solve such difficulties for itself. International treaties may indeed become more frequent, but a finally decisive tribunal of the nations is an impossibility. The appeal to arms will be valid until the end of history, and therein lies the sacredness of war....

[An] essential function of the State is the conduct of war....

Without war no State could be. All those we know of arose through war, and the protection of their members by armed force remains their primary and essential task. War, therefore, will endure to the end of history, as long as there is multiplicity of States. The laws of human thought and of human nature forbid any alternative, neither is one to be wished for. The blind worshipper of an eternal peace falls into the error of isolating the State, or dreams of one which is universal, which we have already seen to be at variance with reason.

Even as it is impossible to conceive of a tribunal above the State, which we have recognized as sovereign in its very essence, so it is likewise impossible to banish the idea of war from the world....

## War Provides Needed Heroes

The grandeur of war lies in the utter annihilation of puny man in the great conception of the State, and it brings out the full magnificence of the sacrifice of fellow-countrymen for one another. In war the chaff is winnowed from the wheat....It is war which fosters the political idealism which the materialist rejects. What a disaster for civilization it would be if mankind blotted its heroes from memory. The heroes of a nation are the figures which rejoice

---

## The State Is Supreme

It must be further understood that all the worth which the human being possesses—all spiritual reality—he possesses only through the State....The State is embodied Morality. It is the ethical spirit which has clarified itself and has taken substantial shape as Will....The State is Mind....The State, being an end in itself, is provided with the maximum of rights against the individual citizens, whose highest duty it is to be members of the State.

Georg Wilhelm Friedrich Hegel, *Philosophy of History.*

---

and inspire the spirit of its youth, and the writers whose words ring like trumpet blasts become the idols of our boyhood and our early manhood. He who feels no answering thrill is unworthy to bear arms for his country. To appeal from this judgment to Christianity would be sheer perversity, for does not the Bible distinctly say that the ruler shall rule by the sword, and again that greater love hath no man than to lay down his life for his friend? To Aryan races, who are before all things courageous, the foolish preaching of everlasting peace has always been vain. They have always been men enough to maintain with the sword what they have attained through the spirit....

## German Devotion to the State

Germany in the nineteenth century has undoubtedly taken the lead in political science, after having followed the foreigner in this domain for two hundred years. The confused course of our history and the repeated violent interruptions which our development has suffered, have at least had the advantage of keeping us from the traditions and prejudices which have so often obscured the political judgment of other peoples.

The complicated functions of our State arise from our place in the world, our history, and our geographical position, all of which enable us to pursue aims which to other nations seem incompatible with each other....

Steadfast loyalty, even though it may be blind, and sometimes politically mischievous, must always remain a proof of the healthy condition of our State and nation.

*"In truth the nations of Europe are a family."*

# Europe: A Family of Nations

William Gladstone

A British prime minister and statesman, William Gladstone (1809-1898) was the leading figure in the movement for political and social reform in nineteenth-century Britain. He exhibited a sincere and altruistic concern for the affairs of humankind and often spoke of injecting politics with the spirit of Christ's Sermon on the Mount. Although he began his public career as an implacable foe of reform, ironically, he ended it as one of the principal agents of the nineteenth-century liberal movement.

As you read, consider the following questions:

1. What criticism does Gladstone make of Germany?
2. How should nations act toward each other, according to the author?
3. What was to be the greatest triumph of Gladstone's time?

William Gladstone, *Gleanings of Past Years*, New York: Charles Scribner's Sons, 1881.

We hear much of the civilisation of the Germans. Let them remember, that Italy has been built up, at least from 1860 onwards, upon the groundwork of the expressed desires of the people of its several portions; that England surrendered the possession of the Ionian Islands in deference to the popular desire, expressed through the representative Chamber, to be united to Greece; that even the Emperor Napoleon took Savoy and Nice under cover of a vote, as to which no one can say that it clearly belied the real public sentiment. This is surely a great advance on the old and cruel practice of treating the population of a civilised European country as mere chattels. Are we to revert to that old practice? Will its revival be in harmony with the feeling, the best feeling, of Europe? Will it conduce to future peace? Can Germany afford, and does she mean, to set herself up above European opinion?...

## Miseries of This Age

Amidst the many additions which this age has contributed to the comfort and happiness of man, it has made some also to his miseries. And among these last is the deplorable discovery of methods by which we can environ peace with many of the worst attributes of war; as, for instance, with its hostility to the regular development of freedom, through the influence of great standing armies, and the prevalence of military ideas; with its hostility to sound and stable government, through crushing taxation, financial embarrassment, and that constant growth of public debt which now, with somewhat rare exceptions, marks the policy of the States of Europe; with the jealous and angry temper, which it kindles between nations; and lastly, with the almost certainty of war itself, as the issue of that state of highly armed preparation, which, we are affectedly told, is the true security for the avoidance of quarrels among men....

In truth the nations of Europe are a family. Some one of them is likely, if not certain, from time to time to be the strongest, either by inherent power or by favouring opportunity. To this strength great influence will attach; and great power over the lot of others. Such influence and power may be abused....

## A New Law of Nations

One accomplishment yet remains needful to enable us to hold without envy our free and eminent position. It is that we should do as we would be done by; that we should seek to found a moral empire upon the confidence of the several peoples, not upon their fears, their passions, or their antipathies. Certain it is that a new law of nations is gradually taking hold of the mind, and coming to sway the practice, of the world; a law which recognises independence, which frowns upon aggression, which favours the pacific, not the bloody settlement of disputes, which aims at permanent and not temporary adjustments; above all, which recognises, as a tribunal of paramount authority, the general judgment of civilised mankind. It has censured the aggression of France; it will censure, if need arise, the greed of Germany.

It is hard for all nations to go astray. Their ecumenical council sits above the partial passions of those, who are misled by interest, and disturbed by quarrel. The greatest triumph of our time, a triumph in a region loftier than that of electricity and steam, will

British Prime Minister William Gladstone warned against the growth of German nationalism.

United Press International, Inc.

be the enthronement of this idea of Public Right, as the governing idea of European policy; as the common and precious inheritance of all lands, but superior to the passing opinion of any. The foremost among the nations will be that one, which by its conduct shall gradually engender in the mind of the others a fixed belief that it is just.

*"The German nation is the only one...inherently strong enough to claim for its national idea the right to participate in the shaping of the world which is to be."*

# Germany: A Nation Above Nations

Paul Rohrbach

Paul Rohrbach was an influential German journalist and avid nationalist. In his book, *The German Idea in the World*, written prior to World War I (1912), he celebrates the alleged superiority of German culture and advocates a worldwide policy of political expansion.

As you read, consider the following questions:

1. What is the German idea, according to the author?
2. What does the author believe should be Germany's role in the world?

Paul Rohrbach, *German World Policies*, New York: Macmillan, 1915.

In speaking of the German idea in the world we mean the ideal force of Germanism as a formative power in relation to the present and future happenings of the world. We start very consciously with the conviction that we have been placed in the arena of the world in order to work out moral perfection, not only for ourselves, but for all mankind.

We believe that this principle and no other governs the continuous selection of the fittest of the peoples, and we are thinking of those who have actually contributed their part to the advance of human progress by placing upon the world the impress of their own national idea. History teaches us that this has often happened without the possession of an exceptionally powerful political empire....

## Germany's Role in the World

It is not necessary to claim for the German idea that it will exist like the Roman either as the mistress of the world or not at all, but it is right to say that it will exist only as the co-mistress of the culture of the world, or it will not exist at all. The Anglo-Saxons have spread over such vast expanses that they seem to be on the point of assuming the cultural control of the world, thanks to their large numbers, their resources and their inborn strength. Russia, which is the largest and most populous non-Anglo-Saxon political entity, is bereft of its former world-embracing political prospects because of its inner lack of culture and its dissensions. France, the rival of England on either side of the ocean in the 18th century, and its superior in its general influence on the culture of the world, has voluntarily withdrawn from the competition of the world powers owing to the moral decline of her people who have condemned themselves to a numerically insufficient progeny. The German nation is the only one which has sufficiently developed by the side of the Anglo-Saxons, and is, moreover, numerically and inherently strong enough to claim for its national idea the right to participate in the shaping of the world which is to be.

The correct interpretation of this proposition implies that we shall be able to maintain our power only if we continue to spread the German idea. We may not cease nor stop, nor even grant a temporary restriction of our sphere of influence, for we have only these alternatives, either to sink back to the level of one of the territorial people, or to fight for a place by the side of the Anglo-Saxons. We are like the tree rooted in the cleft rock. We may press the rock asunder and grow, or the resistance is so great that we are stunted for lack of food....

## Germany's Fate Is England

The German idea, therefore, can only live and increase, if its material foundations, viz., the number of Germans, the prosperity of Germany and the number and size of our world-interests continue to increase. As these foundations continue to grow they compel the Anglo-Saxons to make their decision between the following two propositions: Will they reconcile themselves to seeing our interests in the world maintain themselves by the side of their own, and come to an agreement with us concerning them? Or will they fight, with force of arms, to remain the sole mistress of the world? If they choose the first proposition, they do so because of our strength. If they choose the latter, it will depend on our strength whether we conquer, or surrender, or hold our own.

---

## The Chosen People

Remember, the German people are the chosen of God. On me the German Emperor, the spirit of God has descended. I am His sword, His weapon, and His vice-regent....Germany must have her place in the sun.

Kaiser Wilhelm II, to his soldiers on August 4, 1914.

---

Germany's fate is England. The man who has studied the progress of the world during the last hundred years, and who knows something of the world today from his own observation, knows that there is only one important national-political question: "Is the Anglo-Saxon type destined to gain the sole dominion in those parts of the world where things are still in the process of development, or will there be sufficient scope also for the German idea to take part in the shaping of the culture of the world on both sides of the ocean?"

# Understanding Words in Context

Readers occasionally come across words which they do not recognize. And frequently, because they do not know a word or words, they will not fully understand the passage being read. Obviously, the reader can look up an unfamiliar word in a dictionary. However, by carefully examining the word in the context in which it is used, the word's meaning can often be determined. A careful reader may find clues to the meaning of the word in surrounding words, ideas, and attitudes.

Below are excerpts from the viewpoints in this chapter. In each excerpt, one or two words are printed in italics. Try to determine the meaning of each word by reading the excerpt. Under each excerpt you will find four definitions for the italicized word. Choose the one that is closest to your understanding of the word.

Finally, use a dictionary to see how well you have understood the words in context. It will be helpful to discuss with others the clues which helped you decide on each word's meaning.

1. Natural divisions, the innate spontaneous tendencies of the people, will replace the *ARBITRARY* divisions sanctioned by bad governments.

   *ARBITRARY* means:
   a) natural
   b) random
   c) long
   d) closed

2. If the state neglects its strength in order to promote the idealistic goals of man, it *REPUDIATES* its own nature and perishes.

   *REPUDIATES* means:
   a) smells
   b) publishes
   c) calls
   d) rejects

3. Legal sovereignty is so rooted in the State's nature that it may be said to be its very standard and *CRITERION*.

*CRITERION* means:
a) characteristic
b) criticism
c) authority
d) trick

4. The blind worshipper of an eternal peace falls into the error of isolating the State, or dreams of one which is universal, which we have already seen to be at *VARIANCE* with reason.

*VARIANCE* means:
a) variety
b) disagreement
c) home
d) rhythm

5. England surrendered the possession of the Ionian Islands in *DEFERENCE TO* the islanders' popular desire to be united to Greece.

*DEFERENCE TO* means:
a) madness for
b) respect for
c) protest against
d) action against

6. One accomplishment yet remains needful to enable us to hold without envy our free and *EMINENT* position.

*EMINENT* means:
a) highest
b) uneasy
c) angry
d) motivated

7. A new law of nations is gradually taking hold of the mind; a law which frowns upon aggression, which favours the *PACIFIC*, not the bloody settlement of disputes.

*PACIFIC* means:
a) seagoing
b) peaceable
c) close
d) foolish

8. We are like the tree rooted in the split rock. We may press the rock *ASUNDER* and grow, or the resistance is so great that we are stunted for lack of food.

*ASUNDER* means:
a) loudly
b) together
c) happily
d) apart

# Bibliography

The following list of books, pamphlets and periodical articles deals with the subject matter of this chapter.

D. Beales — *The Risorgimento and the Unification of Italy.* White Plains, NY: Longman Inc., 1982.

Charles F. Detzell — *The Unification of Italy, 1859-1861, Cavour, Mazzini, or Garibaldi?* Melbourne, FL: Krieger Publishing Co., 1976.

Karl W. Deutsch — *Nationalism and Social Communication: An Inquiry into the Foundations of Nationality.* Cambridge: Technology Press, 1953.

Carole Fink — *German Nationalism and the European Response 1890-1945.* Norman, OK: University of Oklahoma Press, 1985.

Theodore S. Hamerow — *Social Foundations of German Unification, 1858-1871.* Princeton, NJ: Princeton University Press, 1969.

Carleton J.H. Hayes — *The Historical Evolution of Modern Nationalism.* New York: Richard B. Smith, 1931.

Georg Wilhelm Friedrich Hegel — *Lectures on the Philosophy of History.* J. Sibree (trans.), London: G. Bell and Sons, 1890.

Friedrich O. Hertz — *Nationality in History and Politics: A Study of the Psychology and Sociology of National Sentiment and Character.* Oxford: Clarendon Press, 1944.

Hans Kohn — *Nationalism and Realism: 1852-1879.* New York: Van Nostrand Reinhold Company, 1968.

Hans Kohn — *Prophets and Peoples: Studies in Nineteenth Century Nationalism.* New York: Macmillan, 1946.

Rosa Luxemberg — *The National Question: Selected Writings.* New York: Monthly Review Press, 1976.

Louis L. Snyder — *The Dynamics of Nationalism: Readings in Its Meaning and Development.* Princeton, NJ: D. Van Nostrand Company, 1964.

Louis L. Snyder — *Macronationalisms: A History of the Pan-Movements.* Westport, CT: Greenwood Press, 1984.

# Twentieth-Century Nationalism: The Roots of Conflict

# Introduction

Rampant nationalism has cursed the twentieth century with a long series of conflicts great and small, foreign and domestic. World Wars I and II, more than a score of civil wars, and several instances of limited big power interventionism, all can be traced to conflicting nationalistic aspirations. Even the unsuccessful popular revolution in Hungary (1956) and the ill-fated movement for constitutional reform in Czechoslovakia (1968) have exposed as myth the belief in a cooperative and dedicated supranational communist movement.

The following viewpoints are meant to illustrate the variety and nature of twentieth-century nationalism. In each case, ethnic, religious and racial differences have served as the convenient banners under which the adversaries could rally. In the Balkans, the struggle involved Slav and Teuton, in Israel, Moslem and Jew, and in South Africa, black and white. Yet each of these seemingly unrelated conflicts have originated from fundamental differences in the historical and cultural traditions of the groups involved. And to the misfortune of the combatants and innocents concerned, each derives its sustenance from hatred and strife.

*"We extend our suzerainty [rule] over Bosnia and Herzegovina, and it is our will that the order of succession of our House be extended to these lands also."*

# The Annexation of Bosnia-Herzegovina

Emperor Francis Joseph I

The nationalistic aspirations of Slavic Serbia were one of the underlying causes of World War I. A sovereign nation since 1804, Serbia long entertained the notion of territorial expansion in the Balkan Peninsula of Europe. Its ultimate goal was a pan-Serbian state which might also include other Slavic speaking peoples of the Balkans. Austria-Hungary, however, conspired to thwart Serbia's ambitions. The presence of twenty-three million disenfranchised Slavs in its own Empire was largely responsible for Austria-Hungary's policy of containment; a large and powerful Serbia would only breed discontent and possible revolution among the hapless Slavs of Austria-Hungary.

In 1908, Austria-Hungary sought to prevent further threats from Serbian nationalists by annexing Bosnia-Herzegovina, a Balkan state it had occupied since 1878. Serbia, believing Bosnia-Herzegovina and its large Serbian population to be its natural preserve, was thoroughly infuriated by the annexation. In the face of a militarily more powerful foe, its response was a carefully coordinated policy of subversion aimed at politically weakening Austria-Hungary. The proliferation of secret societies sponsoring

J.H. Robinson and Charles Beard, editors, *Readings in Modern European History, Vol. II*, Lexington, MA: Ginn & Company, 1909.

Archduke Francis Ferdinand and his wife Sophie, minutes before the assassination.

sabotage, assassinations and revolutionary activity among "captive" Slavs were to serve that policy.

On June 28, 1914, Archduke Francis Ferdinand, the heir to the Austro-Hungarian throne, was murdered by a member of the Serbian Black Hand Society. Using the assassination as a pretext for war and hoping to finally eliminate the Serbian menace, Austria-Hungary declared war on Serbia. The declaration proved the immediate cause of World War I as a system of entangling alliances among the major powers of Europe turned what might have remained a localized affair into a continental conflict.

The following viewpoint is the decree by Emperor Francis Joseph I (1830-1916) announcing the annexation of Bosnia-Herzegovina.

As you read, consider the following questions:

1. What justification does the author give for the annexation of Bosnia-Herzegovina?
2. How does the author believe this annexation will benefit Bosnia-Herzegovina?

We, Francis Joseph, Emperor of Austria, King of Bohemia, and Apostolic King of Hungary, to the inhabitants of Bosnia and Herzegovina:

When a generation ago our troops crossed the borders of your lands, you were assured that they came not as foes, but as friends, with the firm determination to remedy the evils from which your fatherland had suffered so grievously for many years. This promise given at a serious moment has been honestly kept. It has been the constant endeavor of our government to guide the country by patient and systematic activity to a happier future.

To our great joy we can say that the seed then scattered in the furrows of a troubled soil has richly thrived. You yourselves must feel it a boon that order and security have replaced violence and oppression, that trade and traffic are constantly extending, that the elevating influence of education has been brought to bear in your country, and that under the shield of an orderly administration every man may enjoy the fruits of his labors.

It is the duty of us all to advance steadily along this path. With this goal before our eyes, we deem the moment come to give the inhabitants of the two lands a new proof of our trust in their political maturity. In order to raise Bosnia and Herzegovina to a higher level of political life we have resolved to grant both of those lands constitutional governments that are suited to the prevailing conditions and general interests, so as to create a legal basis for the representation of their wishes and needs. You shall henceforth have a voice when decisions are made concerning your domestic affairs, which, as hitherto, will have a separate administration. But the necessary premise for the introduction of this provincial constitution is the creation of a clear and unambiguous legal status for the two lands.

## A New Order

For this reason, and also remembering the ties that existed of yore between our glorious ancestors on the Hungarian throne and these lands, we extend our suzerainty [rule] over Bosnia and Herzegovina, and it is our will that the order of succession of our House be extended to these lands also. The inhabitants of the two lands thus share all the benefits which a lasting confirmation of the present relation can offer. The new order of things will be a guarantee that civilization and prosperity will find a sure footing in your home.

Inhabitants of Bosnia and Herzegovina:

Among the many cares of our throne, solicitude for your material and spiritual welfare shall not be the last. The exalted idea of equal rights for all before the law, a share in the legislation and administration of the provincial affairs, equal protection for all religious creeds, languages, and racial differences, all these high possessions you shall enjoy in full measure. The freedom of the individual and

Arrest of assassin Gavrillo Princip, whose fatal bullet sparked World War I.

the welfare of the whole will be the aim of our government in the two lands. You will surely show yourselves worthy of the trust placed in you, by attachment and loyalty to us and to our House. And thus we hope that the noble harmony between the prince and the people, that dearest pledge of all social progress, will ever accompany us on our common path.

"Austria is the sower of the hate, through her action against us which forces us to struggle until she is destroyed."

# Serbia's Reply to the Annexation

*Narodna Odbrana*

The founding of the *Narodna Odbrana* (Society of National Defense) was one of the responses of Serbian nationalists to the annexation of Bosnia-Herzegovina. The following viewpoint is the program of the Society in which its rationale, goals and methods are declared.

As you read, consider the following questions:

1. How does the *Narodna Odbrana* describe the actions of Austria?
2. What does it state is the new concept of nationalism?
3. What does the *Narodna Odbrana* believe to be its purpose?

From *Europe in the Nineteenth Century 1815-1914*, edited by Eugene N. Anderson, Stanley J. Pincetl, Jr. and Donald J. Zeigler, copyright © 1961 by the Bobs-Merrill Company, Inc.

The *Narodna Odbrana* maintains that the annexation of Bosnia and Herzegovina is clearly an invasion of our country from the north; thus it regards Austria as our principal and greatest enemy and so represents it to our people. The exposition of this idea is in no way fanaticism or chauvinism but a healthy and entirely understandable task, an elementary duty, a need exactly like that to impress the fact that two times two makes four.

The Serbs have never hated for the mere sake of hating, but they have always loved freedom and independence. We have already said in another place that, just as once the Turks from the south pressed upon us, now the Austrians from the north are coming. If the *Narodna Odbrana* is preaching the need for a struggle with Austria, it is but proclaiming the sacred truth which arises out of our national position. If hate and fanaticism develop, they are but natural phenomena which come as results and not as an end. For us the goal is our existence, our freedom. If hate against Austria breaks out, we are not the ones who have sown it; Austria is the sower of the hate, through her action against us which forces us to struggle until she is destroyed.

## A New Concept of Nationalism

Today everywhere a new concept of nationalism has become prevalent. Nationalism (the feeling of nationality) is no longer a historical or poetical feeling, but the true practical expression of life. Among the French, Germans, and English, and among all other civilized peoples, nationalism has grown into something quite new; in it lies the concept of bread, space, air, commerce, competition in everything. Only among us is it still in the old form; that is, it is the fruit of spiritual suffering rather than of reasonable understanding and national advantage. If we speak of freedom and union, we parade far too much the phrases "breaking our chains" and "freeing the slaves"; we call far too much upon our former Serbian glory and think too little of the fact that the freeing of subjected areas and their union with Serbia are necessary to our citizens, our merchants, and our peasants on the grounds of the most elementary needs of culture and trade, of food and space. If one were to explain to our sharp-eyed people our national task as one closely connected with the needs of everyday life, our people would take up the work in a greater spirit of sacrifice than is today the case. We must tell our people that the freedom of Bosnia is necessary, not just because of their feeling of sympathy with their brothers who suffer there, but also because of commerce and its connection with the sea; national union is necessary because of the stronger development of a common culture....

Along with the task of explaining to our people the danger threatening us from Austria, the *Narodna Odbrana* has also the other important tasks of explaining to them, while preserving our holy national memories, this new, healthy, fruitful conception of

**The Balkans States of Europe on the eve of World War I.**

nationalism, and of convincing them to work for national freedom and unity....

The change which took place in Serbia after the annexation is in great part due to the efforts of the *Narodna Odbrana.* As a true national defender, our organization will endure to the end; and if the end comes, if a situation obtains like that at the time of the annexation, thanks to its present activity the *Narodna Odbrana* will face the task which it will have to fulfill then with a tenfold greater ability than it had at the time of the annexation. Through its present activity it is preparing itself and the country for the real function for which it has come into being.

---

### Our National Ideal

Article 1. This organisation has been created with the object of realising the national ideal: The union of all the Serbs. All Serbs...and all who are sincerely devoted to this cause, may become members....

Article 3. This organisation bears the name "Union or Death...."

Article 4. To accomplish its task, the organisation...organises revolutionary action in all territories inhabited by Serbs.

Statutes of the Pan-Serbian Black Hand Society (1911).

---

All in all, the *Narodna Odbrana* aims through its work to advance upon the enemy on the day of reckoning with a sound, nationally conscious, and internally reconciled Serbian people, a nation of Sokols, rifle clubs, heroes—in fact, the fear and terror of the enemy—reliant front-rank fighters and executors of Serbia's holy cause.

If this succeeds, all will be well for us; woe to us if we fail.

*"Let the sovereignty be granted us over a portion of the globe large enough to satisfy the rightful requirements of a nation."*

# Palestine: The Jewish Homeland

Theodor Herzl

Theodor Herzl (1860-1904), an Austro-Hungarian Jewish leader, is considered the father of modern Zionism (an international movement for advancing the state of Israel). In the summer of 1895, he wrote his momentous *Der Judenstaat (The Jewish State)* in which he historically evaluated the "Jewish Question" and pleaded the case for a Jewish Homeland. In August 1897, Herzl was influential in convening the first Zionist Congress in Basel where it was declared that Palestine would be the homeland of the Jews. Acknowledging his preeminent role in the Zionist movement, Herzl prophetically said that "at Basel, I founded the Jewish State. If I said this out loud today, I would be greeted by universal laughter. In five years perhaps, and certainly in fifty years, everyone will perceive it." Fifty years later, in 1948, the state of Israel was proclaimed by the Jews in Palestine and accorded *de facto* recognition by the United States.

As you read, consider the following questions:

1. How does Herzl explain anti-Semitism?
2. What does he believe is the grave situation of the Jews?
3. How is the plan for a new Jewish state justified and described?

Theodor Herzl, *The Jewish State*, London: H. Pordes, 1967. Reprinted with permission.

The idea which I have developed in this pamphlet is a very old one: it is the restoration of the Jewish State....

The Jewish question still exists. It would be foolish to deny it. It is a remnant of the Middle Ages, which civilised nations do not even yet seem able to shake off, try as they will. They certainly showed a generous desire to do so when they emancipated us. The Jewish question exists wherever Jews live in perceptible numbers. Where it does not exist, it is carried by Jews in the course of their migrations. We naturally move to those places where we are not persecuted, and there our presence produces persecution. This is the case in every country, and will remain so, even in those highly civilised—for instance, France—till the Jewish question finds a solution on a political basis. The unfortunate Jews are now carrying Anti-Semitism into England; they have already introduced it into America.

## Age Old Anti-Semitism

I believe that I understand Anti-Semitism, which is really a highly complex movement. I consider it from a Jewish standpoint, yet without fear or hatred. I believe that I can see what elements there are in it of vulgar sport, of common trade jealousy, of inherited prejudice, of religious intolerance, and also of pretended self-defence. I think the Jewish question is no more a social than a religious one, notwithstanding that it sometimes takes these and other forms. It is a national question, which can only be solved by making it a political world-question to be discussed and settled by the civilised nations of the world in council.

We are a people—one people.

We have honestly endeavoured everywhere to merge ourselves in the social life of surrounding communities and to preserve only the faith of our fathers. We are not permitted to do so. In vain are we loyal patriots, our loyalty in some places running to extremes; in vain do we make the same sacrifices of life and property as our fellow-citizens; in vain do we strive to increase the fame of our native land in science and art, or her wealth by trade and commerce. In countries where we have lived for centuries we are still cried down as strangers, and often by those whose ancestors were not yet domiciled in the land where Jews had already made experience of suffering....If we could only be left in peace.

But I think we shall not be left in peace.

Oppression and persecution cannot exterminate us. No nation on earth has survived such struggles and sufferings as we have gone through. Jew-baiting has merely stripped off our weaklings; the strong among us were invariably true to their race when persecution broke out against them....

Old prejudices against us still lie deep in the hearts of the people. He who would have proofs of this need only listen to the people where they speak with frankness and simplicity: proverb and fairytale are both Anti-Semitic. A nation is everywhere a great child, which can certainly be educated; but its education would, even in most favourable circumstances, occupy such a vast amount of time that we could, as already mentioned, remove our own difficulties by other means long before the process was accomplished....

## The Grave Situation of the Jews

No one can deny the gravity of the situation of the Jews. Wherever they live in perceptible numbers, they are more or less persecuted. Their equality before the law, granted by statute, has become practically a dead letter. They are debarred from filling even moderately high positions, either in the army, or in any public or private capacity. And attempts are made to thrust them out of business also: "Don't buy of Jews!"

---

## A Jewish Homeland

His Majesty's Government view with favour the establishment in Palestine of a national home for the Jewish people, and will use their best endeavours to facilitate the achievement of this object, it being clearly understood that nothing shall be done which may prejudice the civil and religious rights of existing non-Jewish communities in Palestine, or the rights and political status enjoyed by Jews in any other country.

A letter from Lord Balfour, former British prime minister sent on November 2, 1917, to Lord Rothschild, a leading British Zionist.

---

Attacks in Parliaments, in assemblies, in the Press, in the pulpit, in the streets, on journeys—for example, their exclusion from certain hotels—even in places of recreation, become daily more numerous: the form of persecution varying according to the countries and social circles in which they occur. In Russia, impositions are levied on Jewish villages; in Roumania, a few persons are put to death; in Germany, they get a good beating occasionally; in Austria, Anti-Semites exercise terrorism over all public life; in Algeria, there are travelling agitators; in Paris, the Jews are shut out of the so-called best social circles and excluded from clubs. Shades of anti-Jewish feeling are innumerable. But this is not to be an attempt to make out a doleful category of Jewish hardships; it is futile to linger over details, however painful they may be....

We are one people—our enemies have made us one in our despite, as repeatedly happens in history. Distress binds us together, and, thus united, we suddenly discover our strength. Yes, we are strong enough to form a State, and, indeed, a model State. We possess all human and material resources necessary for the purpose....

Let the sovereignty be granted us over a portion of the globe large enough to satisfy the rightful requirements of a nation; the rest we shall manage for ourselves.

The creation of a new State is neither ridiculous nor impossible. We have in our day witnessed the process in connection with nations which were not in the bulk of the middle class, but poorer, less educated, and consequently weaker than ourselves. The Governments of all countries scourged by Anti-Semitism will be keenly interested in assisting us to obtain the sovereignty we want.

The plan, simple in design, but complicated in execution, will be carried out by two agencies: The Society of Jews and the Jewish Company.

The Society of Jews will do the preparatory work in the domains of science and politics, which the Jewish Company will afterwards practically apply.

The Jewish Company will see to the realisation of the business interests of departing Jews, and will organise commerce and trade in the new country....

## Palestine: The Jewish Homeland

Those Jews who fall in with our idea of a State will attach themselves to the Society, which will thereby be authorised to confer and treat with Governments in the name of our people. The Society will thus be acknowledged in its relations with Governments as a State-creating power. This acknowledgment will practically create the State.

Should the Powers declare themselves willing to admit our sovereignty over a neutral piece of land, then the Society will enter into negotiations for the possession of this land. Here two territories come under consideration, Palestine and Argentina. In both countries important experiments in colonisation have been made, though on the mistaken principle of a gradual infiltration of Jews. An infiltration is bound to end badly. It continues till the inevitable moment when the native population feels itself threatened, and forces the Government to stop a further influx of Jews. Immigration is consequently futile unless based on an assured supremacy.

The Society of Jews will treat with the present masters of the land, putting itself under the protectorate of the European Powers, if they prove friendly to the plan. We could offer the present possessors of the land enormous advantages, take upon ourselves part of the public debt, build new roads for traffic, which our presence in the country would render necessary, and do many other things. The creation of our State would be beneficial to adjacent countries, because the cultivation of a strip of land increases the value of its surrounding districts in innumerable ways....

Shall we choose Palestine or Argentina...?

Palestine is our ever-memorable historic home. The very name of Palestine would attract our people with a force of marvellous

The roots of genocide: Polish Jews rounded up by Nazi storm troopers, 1939.

United Press International, Inc.

potency....We should there form a portion of the rampart of Europe against Asia, an outpost of civilisation as opposed to barbarism. We should as a neutral State remain in contact with all Europe, which would have to guarantee our existence. The sanctuaries of Christendom would be safeguarded by assigning to them an extra-territorial status such as is well known to the law of nations. We should form a guard of honour about these sanctuaries, answering for the fulfillment of this duty with our existence. This guard of honour would be the great symbol of the solution of the Jewish Question after eighteen centuries of Jewish suffering.

*"We have said that the Arab countries belong to the Arabs and that benefits therefrom must accrue to them."*

# Palestine: The Arab Homeland

First Arab Students' Congress

Since its inception in 1948, the history of the state of Israel has been one of episodic warfare between Arabs and Jews. The Zionist argument of ancient historic rights to the land is rejected by the Arabs who often claim a more ancient heritage. The problem has been exacerbated by the displacement of several million homeless Palestinian refugees and by the involvement of the major world powers. Anticipating the contemporary Middle Eastern dilemma, many Arab groups began espousing Arab nationalism prior to 1948 and depicting Zionists as the enemies of the Arab peoples. In December 1938, a group of Arab students met in Brussels, Belgium and drafted the following manifesto.

As you read, consider the following questions:

1. How is an Arab defined by the authors?
2. What do the authors believe is the new Arab renaissance?
3. Why, according to the authors, are Jews considered a problem?

Sylvia G. Haim, editor, *Arab Nationalism*, Berkeley: University of California Press, 1962. Copyright © 1962 by The Regents of the University of California; reprinted by permission of the University of California Press.

I am an Arab, and I believe that the Arabs constitute one nation. The sacred right of this nation is to be sovereign in her own affairs. Her ardent nationalism drives her to liberate the Arab homeland, to unite all its parts, and to found political, economic, and social institutions more sound and more compatible than the existing ones. The aim of this nationalism is to raise up the standard of living and to increase the material and the spiritual good of the people; it also aspires to share in working for the good of the human collectivity; it strives to realize this by continuous work based on national organization.

I pledge myself to God, that I will strive in this path to my utmost, putting the national interest above any other consideration.

## Who Are the Arabs?

*The Arabs:* All who are Arab in their language, culture, and loyalty [defined in a footnote as "national feeing"], those are the Arabs. The Arab is the individual who belongs to the nation made up of those people.

*The Arab Homeland:* It is the land which has been, or is, inhabited by an Arab majority, in the above sense, in Asia and Africa. As such it is a whole which cannot be divided or partitioned. It is a sacred heritage no inch of which may be trifled with. Any compromise in this respect is invalid and is national treason.

*Arab Nationalism:* It is the feeling for the necessity of independence and unity which the inhabitants of the Arab lands share. [A footnote adds: "The Arab emigrants abroad are included in this definiton."] It is based on the unity of the homeland, of language, culture, history, and a sense of the common good.

*The Arab Movement:* It is the new Arab renaissance which pervades the Arab nation. Its motive force is her glorious past, her remarkable vitality and the awareness of her present and future interests. This movement strives continuously and in an organized manner toward well-defined aims. These aims are to liberate and unite the Arab homeland, to found political, economic, and social organizations more sound than the existing ones, and to attempt afterward to work for the good of the human collectivity and its progress. These aims are to be realized by definite means drawn from the preparedness of the Arabs and their particular situation, as well as from the experience of the West. They will be realized without subscribing to any particular creed of the modern Western ones such as Facism, Communism, or Democracy.

*The Arab National Idea:* It is a national idea which proscribes the existence of racial, regional, and communal fanaticisms. It respects the freedom of religious observance, and individual freedoms such as the freedom of opinion, work, and assembly, unless they conflict with the public good. The Arab national idea cannot be contradictory to the good of real racial and religious minorities; it aims rather at treating all sincere patriots on the principle of equality of rights and duties.

We have said that the Arab countries belong to the Arabs and that benefits therefrom must accrue to them. By Arabs we mean those whom the political report has included under this appellation. As for those elements who are not Arabized and who do not intend to be Arabized but are, rather, intent on putting obstacles in the way of the Arab nation, they are foreign to the Arab nation. The most prominent problem of this kind is that of the Jews in Palestine.

## Arabs Preceded Jews

The argument of the Jews with respect to their rights in Palestine, which is based on their immigration into it two thousand years ago, is "an argument not worthy of consideration or attention," as is textually recorded in the report of the King Crane Commission which came to Palestine in 1919 to ascertain the wishes of the population in Syria and Lebanon. And this argument, supposing that it were valid, is rather in favor of the Arabs than of the Jews, because the Arabs preceded the Jews in Palestine. Robinson, in his book *The History of Israel*, has written about the Arabs of Palestine. "They migrated into Palestine three thousand years before the birth of Christ, coming from the Arabian Peninsula; in spite of this their features and their looks are still apparent in the physiognomy of their descendants." Add to this the fact that the Arab element in Palestine was able in some regions to preserve its independence continuously, even during the golden age of the Jews, so that when the Jewish conquerors were gradually evacuated from Palestine the region came within the zone of influence of the Arab states, until finally it became purely Arab after the great Arab upsurge through Islam.

Muhammad Jamil Baihum, "Arabism and Jewry in Syria."

If we looked at the Jews in Palestine from an economic angle we would find that their economy is totally incompatible with the Arab economy. The Jews are attempting to build up a Jewish state in Palestine and to bring into this state great numbers of their kind from all over the world. Palestine is a small country, and they will therefore have to industrialize it so that this large number of inhabitants can find subsistence. And in order to make their industry a success they will have to find markets for their products. For this they depend on the Arab market; their products will therefore flood the Arab countries and compete with Arab industries....

Moreover, Palestine, placed as it is between the Arab countries in Asia and Africa, occupies an important position in land, sea, and air communications. A foreign state in Palestine will impede these communications and have a harmful effect on commerce. And even if the Jews in Palestine presented no danger other than the economic, this would be enough for us to oppose them and to put an end to their intrigues.

> *"The problem in South Africa is basically not one of race, but of nationalism."*

# South Africa: The Case for the White Afrikaners

Roelof F. Botha

The apartheid policy of the government of South Africa has received worldwide condemnation. The white minority government has been accused of callous racism for its efforts to exclude the black majority in South Africa from active participation in that nation's political processes. However, supporters of apartheid claim that the government's policy is nationalistic, not racial. The South African whites (called Afrikaners), it is argued, have inhabited the country for over 300 years and majority rule would probably deny them virtually all rights in their homeland. The following viewpoint offers a brief historical and contemporary overview of the South African "problem" and attempts both to explain and justify the official Afrikaner position.

As you read, consider the following questions:

1. What are some of Mr. Botha's arguments that explain why South Africa has a right to exist as a white African nation?
2. What are some of the strengths and weaknesses of these arguments? What are the reasons for your choices?

Roelof F. Botha, "Why South Africa Has a Right to Exist as a White African Nation," *Intellect*, August 1977. Reprinted with permission.

The South African Scene is observed from many angles abroad and from differing points of view. In general, a majority of commentators proceed from the same assumption—the policy of the South African government is wrong. It is, of course, relatively easy to condemn a policy as unjust without offering an alternative which is more just.

Take, for instance, the fashionable concept of majority rule, which is proffered by many as a miraculous cure for all the ills of my country. In how many of the countries of the world does one find majority rule in the sense in which Americans understand that concept? Most Americans may agree that one of the most important principles of morality is the application of its norms and demands on an equal basis to all. Morality, by its very nature, can not be selective. How many who demand majority rule for South Africa in the context of American democracy are willing to guarantee to South Africans similar rights? I say, if you can not give the guarantee, do not make the demand.

I do not deny the existence of problems in South Africa or dispute the need for change in my country, but I do say that much of the information on my country is completely unsubstantiated, unbelievably one-sided and distorted, and lacking in perspective. The picture which more than often emerges of South Africa in the outside world, and also in the U.S., is one of unmitigated racism and inhumanity against black South Africans. The impression is being created that everything the South African government does is inherently evil, that the South African government degrades the black man, that the black South African has no political rights, and that the object of the South African government is the perpetual entrenchment of white superiority. This is just not so.

## Historical Perspective

Let me briefly give some historical perspective to indicate the dimensions of our situation.

The South African policy of multinational development goes back 300 years to the arrival of the first white settlers. Throughout the two centuries which followed the convergence on South Africa of the white people by sea and the blacks overland from the areas to the north, the over-all tendency was not only for the whites, but also the various black peoples, to settle in distinct parts of the country. It was during this time that the framework for the homelands policy came into being naturally and historically as each area evolved its own institutions of government, systems of land tenure, traditions, cultures, languages, and economies. In South Africa, the disparities among a heterogenous black population which existed 300 years ago did not come about as a result of Prime Minister Vorster's policies.

The divisions in South African society are of a natural and historical origin of sociological affinity. The choice lay between the

56

relative merits of recognizing the existing political, geographic, and cultural divisions, or attempting to eliminate them and force all the various societies into one artificial unity. The tragic experiences of other parts of the world in attempting to enforce the unity of diversities encourage little optimism in South Africa that the attempt would have any greater chances of success there. A more likely result would be the transfer of political power from one group to another, rather than the radical redistribution of power which critics of South Africa suggest will satisfy their basic criterion of significant change.

## Nationalism and Apartheid

At the root of the separate development program lies the nationalism...of the Afrikaner (White South African)....It is indeed an error to see apartheid as expressive only of an attitude of the white man toward the black. For nationalism as such is not a question of color feeling, and it is nationalism, rather than racialism, that the honest inquirer has basically to comprehend.

Charles A. W. Manning, *Foreign Affairs*, October, 1964.

A development with profound implications for the international political order was the emergence of a deeply felt African nationalism. It must, however, not be forgotten that, over a period of 300 years of constant struggle towards untrammeled independence, the whites of South Africa have evolved their own nationalism, which they will not abdicate. Any just solution must therefore accommodate both black and white nationalisms. Attempts by either nationalism to dominate or overthrow the other will be resisted and could, if alternatives are not found, lead to a conflict with awesome consequences, not only for black and white in South Africa, but further afield....This the South African government wishes to avoid. Its detractors are, in fact, wittingly or unwittingly inviting such a struggle—and, thus, courting disaster.

## Judging South Africa's Policies

Important changes have been introduced in South Africa to improve relations between black and white. More will be introduced. The significance of these changes are seldom correctly assessed. Indeed, they are often rejected by our critics on the grounds that they have no direct bearing on the political power structure. This is precisely where the greatest misunderstanding arises. Critics of the South African government refuse to admit that a just political dispensation can be achieved in South Africa by a division of political power which can accommodate black and white nationalisms, while, at the same time, introducing far-reaching or significant changes in discriminatory measures based on color.

In expressing judgment on the implementation of South Africa's policy it also is important to know that:

• Hundreds of thousands of black workers from other countries of Africa voluntarily come to South Africa for employment, many of them entering the country illegally for that purpose. The average industrial wages for blacks in South Africa are 80% higher than in Ghana, which has one of the highest wage structures in Africa.

• The per capita income of Johannesburg blacks more than doubled between 1970 and 1975. In the same period, white per capita income increased by 58%.

• The consumer market of Johannesburg blacks was worth $750,000,000 in 1975. This compares with independent Botswana's Gross National Product of $175,000,000 in 1973 with a population of about half that of the blacks of Johannesburg.

• The income of black family units in Johannesburg increased from about $1,200 in 1970 to about $2,620 in 1975. The equivalent in purchasing power in the U.S. would be roughly two-and-a-half times these amounts.

• Hundreds of millions of dollars are spent in South Africa to provide free or virtually free medical services to blacks....

• The combined rate of population growth of the black peoples of South Africa is 3.23%—the highest in Africa.

• More than 21% of the total black population of South Africa is attending school, which amounts to more than 4,000,000 pupils. This compares favorably not only with the figures of 10% for the rest of Africa, but also with those for many European and other countries. Of even greater significance is the phenomenal increase in black school attendance at the secondary level....

In contrast to the lack of press freedom in many countries of the world, a large and influential section of the press vigorously criticizes the policies of the South African government daily. Opposition is not limited to the press and is frequently expressed by black leaders in South Africa. No action is or can be taken under South African law against opponents and critics as long as their opposition is conducted in a constitutional manner....

White South Africans did not conquer black nations and did not steal their land. The areas occupied by the White Trekkers (pioneers) to the north were for the most part completely uninhabited due to what the blacks still call the "mfekane" or "crushing."

## The Right to Exist

White South Africans are an African nation and insist on the right to exist and govern themselves. However, what is apparently demanded from them is that they should willingly accept their own demise in their own country because they wish to preserve that which is dear to them as a nation. Where is the morality in this type of demand? Where is the equality and justice in the clamor for censuring South Africa on account of alleged inequalities when the overwhelming majority of the peoples of the world know no freedom, no security of person, and never participate in any process to elect their governments? In contrast, South Africa's principal aim is to allow each nation, black and white, to achieve sovereign independence.

The problem in South Africa is basically not one of race, but of nationalism, which is a worldwide problem. There is a white nationalism and there are several black nationalisms. These are realities. A just and viable solution of the problems must cater to the aims of all these nationalisms.

One of the black nations, Transkei, was established as a state, with full sovereignty, on Oct. 26, 1976. That it has not been recognized as a full member of the family of nations derogates not at all from the physical fact that it is an African nation, formerly subject to white rule, now fully in command of its own destiny,

South African Roelof F. Botha confers with Rhodesian Prime Minister Ian Smith.

having achieved its independence through peaceful, constitutional means. Withholding recognition of Transkei is based on the application of double standards. Transkei meets the criteria of statehood more convincingly than a few dozen states that are now members of the UN—*e.g.,* size of land area and population, per capita income, budget, educational advancement, economic base, and political system.

To conclude, the only choice we have before us in Southern Africa is either to continue on the sterile course of confrontation and recrimination or to make a sincere endeavor to come to an understanding with one another and to listen to the other man's point of view with an open mind. Communication or confrontation—that is our choice.

*"The lack of human dignity experienced by Africans is the direct result of the policy of White supremacy."*

# South Africa: The Case for the Black Africans

Nelson Mandela

Nelson Mandela is a leader of the African National Congress, the oldest nationalist group in Africa. In 1960, he was sentenced by the apartheid South African government to five years imprisonment for incitement to strike and traveling without a valid passport. In October 1963, a group of black nationalists, who were intimates of Mandela, were arrested and charged with sabotage and conspiracy to overthrow the government by revolution. Mandela was taken from prison and made to stand trial as one of the accused. On April 20, 1964, he dramatically opened the case for the defense with the following speech. Ultimately sentenced to life imprisonment, Nelson Mandela remains a rallying figure for black South Africans.

As you read, consider the following questions:

1. Why is South Africa a land of extreme contrasts, according to the author?
2. How does the author believe white supremacy affects Africans?

Nelson Mandela, *No Easy Walk to Freedom*, London: Heinemann, 1965. Reprinted with permission.

South Africa is the richest country in Africa, and could be one of the richest countries in the world. But it is a land of extremes and remarkable contrasts. The Whites enjoy what may well be the highest standard of living in the world, whilst Africans live in poverty and misery. Forty per cent of the Africans live in hopelessly overcrowded and, in some cases, drought-stricken Reserves, where soil erosion and the overworking of the soil make it impossible for them to live properly off the land. Thirty per cent are labourers, labour tenants, and squatters on White farms and work and live under conditions similar to those of the serfs of the Middle Ages. The other 30 per cent live in towns where they have developed economic and social habits which bring them closer in many respects to White standards. Yet most Africans, even in this group, are impoverished by low incomes and high cost of living....

## Disease Rate and Educational Standards

Poverty goes hand in hand with malnutrition and disease. The incidence of malnutrition and deficiency diseases is very high amongst Africans. Tuberculosis, pellagra, kwashiorkor, gastro-enteritis, and scurvy bring death and destruction of health. The incidence of infant mortality is one of the highest in the world. According to the Medical Officer of Health for Pretoria, tuberculosis kills forty people a day (almost all Africans), and in 1961 there were 58,491 new cases reported. These diseases not only destroy the vital organs of the body, but they result in retarded mental conditions and lack of initiative, and reduce powers of concentration. The secondary results of such conditions affect the whole community and the standard of work performed by African labourers.

The complaint of Africans, however, is not only that they are poor and the Whites are rich, but that the laws which are made by the Whites are designed to preserve this situation. There are two ways to break out of poverty. The first is by formal education, and the second is by the worker acquiring a greater skill at his work and thus higher wages. As far as Africans are concerned, both these avenues of advancement are deliberately curtailed by legislation.

The present Government has always sought to hamper Africans in their search for education. One of their early acts, after coming into power, was to stop subsidies for African school feeding. Many African children who attended schools depended on this supplement to their diet. This was a cruel act.

There is compulsory education for all White children at virtually no cost to their parents, be they rich or poor. Similar facilities are not provided for the African children, though there are some who receive such assistance. African children, however, generally have to pay more for their schooling than Whites....

The quality of education is also different. According to the Bantu Educational Journal, only 5,660 African children in the whole of South Africa passed their J.C. in 1962, and in that year only 362 passed matric. This is presumably consistent with the policy of Bantu education about which the present Prime Minister said, during the debate on the Bantu Education Bill in 1953:

> When I have control of Native education I will reform it so that Natives will be taught from childhood to realize that equality with Europeans is not for them....People who believe in equality are not desirable teachers for Natives. When my Department controls Native education it will know for what class of higher education a Native is fitted, and whether he will have a chance in life to use his knowledge.

### White Supremacy and Oppression

The lack of human dignity experienced by Africans is the direct result of the policy of White supremacy. White supremacy implies Black inferiority. Legislation designed to preserve White supremacy entrenches this notion. Menial tasks in South Africa are invariably performed by Africans. When anything has to be carried or cleaned the White man will look around for an African to do it for him, whether the African is employed by him or not. Because of this sort of attitude, Whites tend to regard Africans as a separate breed. They do not look upon them as people with families of their own; they do not realize that they have emotions—that they fall in love like White people do; that they want to be with their wives and children like White people want to be with theirs; that they want to earn enough money to support their families properly, to feed and clothe them and send them to school. And what 'house-boy' or 'garden-boy' or labourer can ever hope to do this?

Pass laws, which to the Africans are among the most hated bits of legislation in South Africa, render any African liable to police surveillance at any time. I doubt whether there is a single African male in South Africa who has not at some stage had a brush with

ONE MAN ONE VOTE WOULD LEAD TO THE DOMINATION OF ONE GROUP OVER THE OTHER

KAL, *The Observer*, London

the police over his pass. Hundreds and thousands of Africans are thrown into jail each year under pass laws. Even worse than this is the fact that pass laws keep husband and wife apart and lead to the breakdown of family life....

## "I Am Prepared to Die"

Africans want to be paid a living wage. Africans want to perform work which they are capable of doing, and not work which the Government declares them to be capable of. Africans want to be allowed to live where they obtain work, and not be endorsed out of an area because they were not born there. Africans want to be allowed to own land in places where they work, and not to be obliged to live in rented houses which they can never call their own. Africans want to be part of the general population, and not confined to living in their own ghettoes. African men want to have their wives and children to live with them where they work, and not be forced into an unnatural existence in men's hostels. African women want to be with their menfolk and not be left permanently widowed in the Reserves. Africans want to be allowed out after eleven o'clock at night and not to be confined to their rooms like little children. Africans want to be allowed to travel in their own country and to seek work where they want to and not where the Labour Bureau tells them to. Africans want a just share in the whole of South Africa; they want security and a stake in society.

Above all, we want equal political rights, because without them our disabilities will be permanent. I know this sounds revolutionary to the Whites in this country, because the majority of voters will be Africans. This makes the White man fear democracy.

But this fear cannot be allowed to stand in the way of the only solution which will guarantee racial harmony and freedom for all. It is not true that the enfranchisement of all will result in racial domination. Political division, based on colour, is entirely artificial and, when it disappears, so will the domination of one colour group by another. The ANC* has spent half a century fighting against racialism. When it triumphs it will not change that policy.

This then is what the ANC is fighting. Their struggle is a truly national one. It is a struggle of the African people, inspired by their own suffering and their own experience. It is a struggle for the right to live.

During my lifetime I have dedicated myself to this struggle of the African people. I have fought against White domination, and I have fought against Black domination. I have cherished the ideal of a democratic and free society in which all persons live together in harmony and with equal opportunities. It is an ideal which I hope to live for and to achieve. But if needs be, it is an ideal for which I am prepared to die.

*ANC—African National Congress, founded in 1912 to defend the rights of the black Africans.

# Recognizing Stereotypes

A stereotype is an oversimplified or exaggerated description of people or things. Stereotyping can be favorable. However, most stereotyping tends to be highly uncomplimentary and, at times, degrading.

Stereotyping grows out of our prejudices. Consider the following example: Ms. Smith believes that all Jewish people cheat to get wealthy. When a Jewish family moves into her neighborhood, she comments to a friend, "They must have cheated a lot of people to buy that house." Ms. Smith does not bother to find out whether the new family worked hard to afford their new house. She judged the Jewish family on the basis of her stereotype rather than on the family members themselves.

The following statements relate to the subject matter in this chapter. Consider each statement carefully. *Mark S for any statement that is an example of stereotyping. Mark N for any statement that is not an example of stereotyping. Mark U if you are undecided about any statement.*

If you are doing this activity as a member of a class or group, compare your answers with those of other class or group members. Be able to defend your answers. You may discover that others will come to different conclusions than you. Listening to the reasons others present for their answers may give you valuable insights in recognizing stereotypes.

If you are reading this book alone, ask others if they agree with your answers. You too will find this interaction very valuable.

S = *stereotype*
N = *not a stereotype*
U = *undecided*

1. The people of Bosnia and Herzegovina will never get over their hatred of Austria.

2. Anyone who is a Serb must love freedom and independence.

3. The state paper maintains that the annexation of Bosnia and Herzegovina is an invasion of our country.

4. I never met an Austrian who didn't sow hate like a farmer sows seed.

5. Today it seems everyone we see embraces a new concept of nationalism.

6. Anti-Semites are the sort who engage in vulgar sport, common trade jealousy, and religious intolerance of all kinds.

7. The "Jewish question" has existed since the Middle Ages.

8. The Jews have migrated more often and in greater numbers than any people in recorded history.

9. Jews are in every way intent on putting obstacles in the way of the Arab nation.

10. Jews will take over Arab markets as they have taken over markets in every other country in the world.

11. Americans agree that the most important principle of morality is the application of its norms and demands on an equal basis to all.

12. Black South Africans have claimed that they have no political rights.

13. The South African policy of multinational development goes back 300 years to the arrival of the first white settlers.

14. Any white South African would rather keep his wealth than see one black South African raise his standard of living.

15. White South African children have compulsory education.

16. South Africans are narrow in their thinking; they can't see beyond the borders of their own country.

17. Black South Africans aren't really human; they don't deserve the same rights that others do.

18. Hundreds and thousands of Africans are thrown into jail each year under pass laws.

19. South Africa is the richest country in Africa.

# Bibliography

The following list of books, periodicals, and pamphlets deals with the subject matter of this chapter.

Edward Alexander — "Liberalism and Zionism," *Commentary*, February 1986.

George Antonius — *The Arab Awakening: The Story of the Arab National Movement*. Philadelphia: Lippincott, 1939.

*Ebony* — "Unity of Blackness," August 1969.

Dorothy A. Faber — "Pros and Cons of Apartheid," *South African Scope*, April 1975.

Nadine Gordimer — "The Just Cause," *The New York Review of Books*, November 7, 1985.

Oscar I. Janowsky — *Foundations of Israel*. New York: D. Van Nostrand Company, 1959.

A. Johnson — "Nationalism in the Middle East," *School and Society*, September 19, 1956.

Hans Kohn — *Pan-Slavism: Its History and Ideology*. New York: Vintage Books, 1960.

Winnie Mandela — *Part of My Soul Went with Him*. New York: Norton, 1985.

Gennady Mikhailov — "Nationalism: Weapon of Psychological Warfare," *New Times*, June 1984.

Lydia Modzhoryan — "Zionism in Crisis," *New Times*, December 1985.

Raymond Pearson — *National Minorities in Eastern Europe, 1848-1944*. New York: St. Martin's Press, 1984.

Harold H. Saunders — "Arabs and Israelis: A Political Strategy," *Foreign Affairs*, Winter 1985/86.

Oliver Tambo — "A South African Fights from Exile," *The New York Times*, December 6, 1985.

U.S. News and World Report — "How to End the Racial Turmoil in South Africa," December 2, 1985.

J. Voster — "South Africa's Side of the Story," *U.S. News and World Report*, July 15, 1968.

Z.A. Zeman — *The Break-up of the Hapsburg Empire: A Study in National and Social Revolution*. New York: Octagon Press, 1977.

# Nationalism and Revolution

# Introduction

In his 1983 book, *Imagined Communities: Reflections on the Origin and Spread of Nationalism,* Benedict Anderson wrote that every successful revolution since World War II has defined itself in nationalist terms. Whether one agrees with Mr. Anderson's interpretation of postwar history or not, nationalism's influence on revolutions should not be ignored. This chapter focuses on three nationalist uprisings. Their chances of succeeding were not good since they were directed against established governments with powerful allies. Thus, while postwar nationalism has often led to successful revolutions, according to Mr. Anderson, it has also led to seemingly suicidal ventures as the viewpoints in this chapter show.

For leader Imre Nagy, his part in the 1956 Hungarian revolution led to his capture, trial, and eventual execution. For many Czechoslovakian intellectuals and writers, their revolutionary activities in 1968 led to unemployment or tedious jobs in the country, and some either emigrated or were arrested. In Japan, Yukio Mishima's attempted nationalist uprising failed miserably. To save face and in hopes of stirring young Japanese to nationalist fervor, he committed ritual suicide in the Japanese samurai tradition. Mishima wished that modern, industrialized Japan had never left its warlord era.

These three attempted revolutions share a common trait—their leaders were convinced they had the proper vision of what their countries should be and they willingly took suicidal risks for their nationalist visions.

*"Guaranteeing our national independence and sovereignty,...alone can be the basis of socialism in our country."*

# Hungarian Nationalism Is Legitimate

Imre Nagy and Béla Kovács (as interviewed by Leslie B. Bain)

The following viewpoint features two Hungarian revolutionary leaders. Part I is an October 28, 1956 radio address by Hungarian Prime Minister Imre Nagy. Hungary, and many other Communist countries, adopted several reforms after Soviet leader Joseph Stalin's death in 1953. Mr. Nagy became prime minister that year, replacing a hard-line Stalinist, Mátyás Rákosi. During the Hungarian revolt, which was started by student protesters, Mr. Nagy renounced the Warsaw Pact and declared Hungary a neutral country. When the Soviets invaded on November 4, 1956 to crush the rebellion, the Nagy government collapsed. Part II is an interview reporter Leslie Bain had with Béla Kovács, a non-Communist Hungarian leader. Mr. Kovács argues that national pride is more important to Hungarians than communism, which is why Hungarian Communists started the revolution.

As you read, consider the following questions:

1. What does Mr. Nagy believe must be the basis for socialism in Hungary?
2. What kind of an economy did Mr. Kovács believe Hungary would have established under Mr. Nagy's leadership?

Imre Nagy, Radio Kossuth, October 28, 1956. Béla Kovács interviewed by Leslie B. Bain, *The Reporter*, December 13, 1956. Both reprinted in *The Hungarian Revolution*, edited by Melvin J. Lasky. New York: Frederick A. Praeger, Inc., 1957.

# I

People of Hungary! Last week, bloody events followed, one after another, with tragic rapidity. The fateful consequences of the horrible mistakes and crimes of the past decade are unfolding before us in the painful events which we are witnessing and in which we are participants. During our thousand-year-old history fate was not sparing in scourging our people and nation, but such a shock as this has perhaps never before afflicted our country.

The Government rejects the view that sees the present formidable popular movement as a counter-revolution. Without doubt, as always happens at the time of great popular movements, in the last few days, evil-doers seized the chance of committing common crimes. It also occurred that reactionary, counter-revolutionary elements joined the movement and tried to make use of events for overthrowing the people's democratic system. But it is also indisputable that in this movement, a great national and democratic movement embracing and unifying all our people, unfolded itself with elementary force. This movement has the aim of guaranteeing our national independence and sovereignty, of advancing the democratization of our social, economic and political life, for this alone can be the basis of socialism in our country.

## Birth of a Government

The grave crimes of the preceding era released this great movement. The situation was aggravated even further by the fact that up to the very last the leadership was unwilling to break totally with its old and criminal policy. This, above all, led to the tragic fratricidal fight in which so many people are dying on both sides.

In the midst of the fighting was born a Government of democratic national unity, independence and socialism, which has become the genuine means for expressing the people's will. This is the firm resolve of the Government: The new Government, relying on the strength and control of the people, and in the hope that it will obtain the full confidence of the people, will immediately begin to realize the people's just demands....

The Government wants to rely, first of all, on the militant Hungarian working class but, naturally, it wants to rely also on the entire Hungarian working people.

The Government strongly supports the worker, peasant and student youth and university students, their activity and initiative; great scope should be secured for them in our purified political life, and it will do its best to see that young people starting their careers should enjoy as good a financial situation as possible. The Government will support the new democratic autonomous bodies created on the initiative of the people and will endeavour to integrate them into the State administration.

In the interest of avoiding further bloodshed and ensuring a peaceful clarification of the situation, the Government has ordered an immediate and general cease-fire. It has instructed the armed forces to open fire only if attacked. At the same time it appeals to all those who took up arms to refrain from all fighting activity and to surrender their arms without delay. For maintaining order and restoring public security, a new security force has been created, at once, from units of the police and Honveds, as well as from the armed platoons of the workers and youth.

---

### Hungarian National Interests

End the massacre of Hungarians in Budapest! Do not believe deceptions! Let them withdraw Soviet troops from Hungary! Strike!...

We too want socialism, but according to our own special Hungarian conditions, which reflect the interests of the Hungarian working class and the Hungarian nation, and our most sacred national sentiments.

From a broadcast on Radio Free Miskolc, Hungary on October 25, 1956.

---

The Hungarian Government has come to an agreement with the Soviet Government that Soviet troops will immediately begin their withdrawal from Budapest and, simultaneously with the establishment of the new security forces, will leave the city's territory.

The Hungarian Government is initiating negotiations to settle relations between the Hungarian People's Republic and the Soviet Union, including the question of the withdrawal of Soviet troops stationed in Hungary. All this is in the spirit of Soviet-Hungarian friendship, equality among socialist countries and national independence.

After the restoration of order we are going to organise a new and single state police force and we shall abolish the State Security Authority. No one who took part in the armed fighting need fear further reprisals....

People of Hungary! In these hours of bitterness and conflict, people are prone to see only the black side of our history during the last 12 years [since communism was established], but we must not allow ourselves to entertain such an unjust view of things. These 12 years mark historic achievements, both lasting and ineffaceable, which have been attained by Hungarian workers, peasants and intellectuals under the leadership of the Hungarian Workers' Party. In this force, the spirit of sacrifice and creative work, our revived people's democracy has the best guarantee of Hungary's future.

## II

Late in the evening of Sunday, November 4—a night of terror in Budapest that no one who lived through it will ever forget—I met

Béla Kovács, one of the leaders of Hungary's short-lived revolutionary government, in a cellar in the city's center....

Kovács, as a Minister of State of the Nagy régime, had started off for the Parliament Building early that morning, but he never reached it. Soviet tanks were there ahead of him. Now he squatted on the floor opposite me, a fugitive from Soviet search squads....

## His "Rehabilitation"

A hunched, stocky man, with a thin mustache and half-closed eyes, Béla Kovács was only a shadow of the robust figure he once had been. Now in his early fifties, he had risen to prominence after the war as one of the top leaders of the Hungarian Independent Smallholders Party. Back in 1947, when Mátyás Rákosi began taking over the government with the support of the Soviet occupation forces, Kovács had achieved fame by being the only outstanding anti-Communist Hungarian leader to defy Rákosi and continue open opposition. His prestige had become so great among the peasantry that at first the Communists had not molested him. But then the Soviets themselves stepped in, arresting him on a trumped-up charge of plotting against the occupation forces and sentencing him to life imprisonment. After eight years in Siberia, Kovács was returned to Hungary and transferred to a Hungarian jail, from which he was released in the spring of 1956, broken in body but not in spirit by his long ordeal. After what was called his "rehabilitation," Kovács was visited by his old enemy Rákosi, who called to pay his respects. Rákosi was met at the door by this message from Kovács: "I do not receive murderers in my home."

## Nagy's Coalition

So long as Nagy's government was still under the thumb of the Communist Politburo, Kovács refused to have anything to do with the new régime. Only in the surge of the late October uprising, when Nagy succeeded in freeing himself from his former associates and cast about to form a coalition government, did Kovács consent to lend his name and immense popularity to it. He himself had not been in Budapest when the revolt broke out, but at his home in Pécs, a southern city near the Yugoslav border. In fact, he told me, he was made a member of the new Nagy government before he had even a chance to say "Yes" or "No," but, understanding the situation and what Nagy was trying to do, he had agreed to go along. The name of Kovács among the Ministers of State was to many Hungarians a guarantee of a new era in which the government would carry out the mandates of the victorious revolution.

At about six o'clock in the morning of November 4, when Soviet tanks were already pouring into the city, Kovács had received a message from Nagy calling an immediate meeting of the Cabinet. When he reached Parliament Square the Russians had already thrown a tight cordon around it. One of Nagy's new Ministers,

Zoltan Tildy, who had been ousted from the Presidency in 1948, came out of the building and told Kovács that he had just negotiated a surrender agreement with the Russians whereby civilians would be permitted to leave the building unmolested in exchange for surrendering the seat of the government. However, Tildy reported, State Minister Istvan Bibo refused to leave and had entrenched himself with a machine gun on the second floor. Tildy begged Kovács to get in touch with Bibo by telephone and order him to leave. Then Tildy himself left.

Freedom fighters, among whom there were many teen-age girls, advance from cover to investigate a stationary tank.

Kovács called Bibo from a nearby phone and tried to persuade him to leave. He was unable to move the aroused Minister, whose argument was that if the Russians moved against him, this would serve as a clear demonstration before the world that Soviet forces had been employed to crush the independent Hungarian government. Bibo declared that the Russians intended to install Janos Kadar and his clique as a new government, and by not yielding, he wanted to demonstrate that the exchange of governments was accomplished by armed force.

I told Kovács that as late as four in the afternoon, I had been in touch with the beleaguered Bibo by telephone. He was still holding out, but an hour later his private line did not answer. By that time Premier Nagy himself was in custody, and the Ministers who had not been arrested were in hiding. Kovács voiced his admiration of both Bibo and the Premier. "My fondest memory of Nagy," he said to me, "will always be his transformation from an easy-going, jolly, studious professor into a flaming revolutionary."

"What do you think caused the Russians to change their tactics and come in again?" I asked Kovács.

## Why the Soviets Invaded

"Two things. First, we went too fast and too far, and the Communists panicked. Second, the Russians felt deeply humiliated." He went on to explain that he felt that all the goals of the revolution could have been attained if there had been a way to slow down the process. In a free election, he estimated, all the left-of-center parties would not command more than thirty per cent of the vote. But a free election was what the Communists were afraid to risk.

"Wouldn't such an election have brought in the extreme Right and possibly a new reign of White Terror?" I asked.

Kovács admitted there might have been a possibility of that, but he was convinced it could have been checked in time. He went on to say that in his estimation there was no chance of reconstituting large land-holdings in the hands of their former owners or of the workers permitting the return of the mines and factories to their former owners. "The economic salvation of Hungary lies in a mixed economy, combining capitalism, state ownership, and co-operatives," he said. Politically, there had been the likelihood of a strongly rightist development, but, in the absence of economic power, after a few short months the extremists would have been silenced....

## Hungarian Neutrality

I asked Kovács whether he felt the Nagy government's declaration of neutrality had aroused the Soviet leaders to action. No, he thought that the decision to crush the Hungarian revolution was taken earlier and independently of it. Obviously the Russians would not have rejoiced at a neutral Hungary, but so long as economic cooperation between the states in the area was assured the Russians and their satellites should not have been too unhappy.

In that regard, Kovács assured me, there was never a thought in the Nagy government of interrupting the economic co-operation of the Danubian states. "It would have been suicidal for us to try tactics hostile to the bloc. What we wanted was simply the right to sell our product to the best advantage of our people and buy our necessities where we could do it most advantageously."

"Then in your estimation there was no reason why the Russians should have come again and destroyed the revolution?"

"None unless they are trying to revert to the old Stalinist days.

But if that is what they really are trying—and at the moment it looks like it—they will fail, even more miserably than before. The tragedy of all this is that they are burning all the bridges which could lead to a peaceful solution."

## No Rapprochement

He went on in the semi-darkness to say that after today there would be no way to bring about a rapprochement between Hungary and the Soviet Union. The wound the Russians were inflicting on Hungary was so deep that it would fester for generations. "Yet we can't pick up Hungary and take it somewhere else. We have to go on living with our ancient neighbours who are now in the Soviet grip."

---

### Prostituted Communism

We have very little to say to the Soviet masters. They have convinced not only the whole world, but also all Communists, that they do not care for Communism, that they simply prostituted Communism...to Russian imperialism.

We also want to speak of the traitors...the Janos Kadars, who play the dirty role of colonial governors....We send them the message that we consider them all traitors to Communism.

From a broadcast on Free Radio Rajk, Hungary on November 5, 1956.

---

We discussed the revolution itself. Kovác's somber eyes lit up. "It has brought modern history to a turning point," he said. "It has exposed totalitarian fallacies more sharply than any event before. Our people were beaten, cowed, and for years lived in abject surrender, yet when the hour struck they all streamed out of their homes, Communists and non-Communists alike, to regain their self-respect by defying their tormentors. And look what happened to the Communist Party! It disappeared overnight—not forced to dissolve, but by common consent! Have you ever heard of a ruling party voting itself out of existence? Once the revolution touched them, all became Hungarians—all except those whose crimes were too many to be forgiven. These are the ones who now serve their Russian masters."...

How much truth was in the Russian assertion that the revolution had become a counter-revolution and that therefore Russian intervention was justified?

### Determined Resistance

"I tell you," said Kovács, "this was a revolution from inside, led by Communists. There is not a shred of evidence that it was otherwise. Communists outraged by their own doings prepared the

76

ground for it and fought for it during the first few days. This enabled us former non-Communist party leaders to come forward and demand a share in Hungary's future. Subsequently this was granted by Nagy, and the Social Democratic, Independent Smallholders, and Hungarian Peasant parties were reconstituted. True, there was a small fringe of extremists in the streets and there was also evidence of a movement which seemed to have ties with the exiled Nazis and Nyilas of former days. But at no time was their strength such as to cause concern. No one in Hungary cares for those who fled to the West after their own corrupt terror régime was finished—and then got their financing from the West. Had there been an attempt to put them in power, all Hungary would have risen instantly...."

"What of the future?" I asked. After some hesitation Kovács said: "All is not lost, for it is impossible for the Russians and their puppets to maintain themselves against the determined resistance of the Hungarians. The day will come when a fateful choice will have to be made: Exterminate the entire population by slow starvation and police terror or else accept the irreducible demand—the withdrawal of Soviet forces from our country."

*"One member of our hotel staff...told us: 'Our workers cannot have had a hand in this looting and rioting. It is fascism raising its head.' "*

# Hungarian Nationalism Is a Fraud

*Pravda* and E.M. Bazarina

The Soviet Union considered the Hungarian revolt a counter-revolutionary coup armed by the West. Soviet reaction can be better understood when put in the context of the Cold War and the extreme hostility and fear the United States and Soviet Union felt toward one another during the 1950s. The Soviet position is explained in the following viewpoint. It includes an October 29, 1956 article in *Pravda*, the official Soviet newspaper, Part I, and a Radio Moscow report E.M. Bazarina made on November 10, 1956, Part II. Both authors argue that Hungarian demonstrations were taken over by a fascist, nationalist underground, supplied by the West. Followers of a former Hungarian dictator, Nicholas Horthy, conducted a reign of "White Terror" which is why the Soviet Union had to intervene.

As you read, consider the following questions:

1. In part I, what groups does *Pravda* argue supported the Hungarian revolution?
2. According to Mr. Bazarina, what two groups tried, in spite of the counterrevolutionaries, to establish order in Budapest during the fighting?
3. What does Mr. Bazarina mean by "White Terror"?

*Pravda*, October 28, 1956.   E.M. Bazarina, Radio Moscow, November 10, 1956. Both reprinted in *The Hungarian Revolution*, edited by Melvin J. Lasky. New York: Frederick A. Praeger, Inc., 1957.

# I

What happened in Hungary? Comrade Janos Kadar characterized these events in his October 25 radio speech as follows: "...The leadership of our party unanimously decided that all possible measures should be taken to repel the armed outbursts against our people's democratic system...." Comrade Imre Nagy speaking over the radio the same day, also indicated that "a handful of counter-revolutionary instigators staged an armed attack against the regime of our People's Republic, and this attack was supported by some sections of the Budapest working people who were dissatisfied with the situation in Hungary."

## Imperialist Interference

This anti-popular adventure was the result of prolonged subversive activity conducted by the imperialist powers with the criminal intent of destroying the people's democracies and restoring the capitalist system in these countries. While the countries of the socialist camp fight consistently with all the power at their command for peaceful coexistence of states with different social and economic systems, for the reduction of international tension and for the strengthening of international co-operation, the imperialist circles of the United States, England, Western Germany, and certain other countries are making every effort to interfere in the affairs of the socialist countries through provocations, subversive activity, and the organization of a counter-revolutionary underground....

Events in Hungary made it crystal clear that a reactionary counter-revolutionary underground, well-armed and thoroughly prepared for decisive action against the people's government, had been organized with outside help. This is borne out by the fact that the rebels acted according to a plan laid out in advance and were led by people experienced in military affairs, namely by officers of the Horthy regime....

## Nationalist Demagogy

Bourgeois propaganda is now trying to present the working people as the pioneers of the armed rising. But surely there is not a single honest person who would dare to equate the Hungarian working people with those people who barbarously set fire to the National Museum and directed their automatic rifles and machine guns against the firemen and soldiers who tried to save art treasures belonging to the Hungarian people? Who would dare to put Hungarian workers on a par with those who burned books in the streets of Budapest, thus reviving a spectacle of medieval obscurantism and Hitlerite vandalism?...

*Trybuna Ludu*, the Polish United Workers' Party newspaper, comments on the events in Hungary as follows: "Unfortunately, organized counter-revolutionary elements, ready to turn the senti-ments of the Hungarian public against the most sacred cause—the cause of socialism—infiltrated the peaceful demonstrations of the Hungarian population. These elements circulated unbridled nationalistic and anti-Soviet demagogic slogans and drew upon the reservoir of the politically backward strata of society. A very dangerous situation resulted which was a threat to the socialist con-quests of the Hungarian working people and of the people's system."

# II

We arrived in Hungary on 19 October with other Soviet tourists. We spent four days touring this beautiful country and were every-where given a most cordial and hearty welcome. On Tuesday, 23 October, on our way to a theatre we saw crowds of people in the streets of Budapest. They were lined up in ranks and carried placards, many of which bore the inscription "Long live Hungary!"...The students together with members of the intelligent-sia and workers were demanding the redress of errors and omis-sions committed by the Hungarian Government. They were legitimate demands....

---

## Enemies of the Hungarian People

The disorders in Budapest and other parts of the country have been used by direct enemies of the Hungarian working people and by their foreign sponsors....

Unfortunately the enemies of the Hungarian people have to a cer-tain extent been successful. A situation is now arising in Hungary which threatens all the achievements of the Hungarian working people during the years of the people's rule. Friends tell the truth to your face, because they want to help and warn their friends against a wrong step.

From a broadcast by V. Kartsev on Radio Moscow, USSR on November 2, 1956.

---

On that first evening I saw from the hotel in which we were stay-ing a man with a rifle appear in the deserted street. He took up a position in one of the drives and, taking careful aim, began shooting out the street lamps. The lamps went out one by one and darkness enveloped the street. What prompted the marksman to do this? Just hooliganism? Hardly. I think he was one of the bright sparks of the reactionary underground who wanted to create confusion and chaos in the city. Quite soon afterwards there were flashes of gun-fire and sounds of battle and we saw wrecked and burning buildings in the streets of Budapest, overturned tram-cars and other vehicles. Firing would die down and then flare up again. Hostile elements were aiming at paralysing the city's life but the workers of Budapest were repelling the rebels. Detachments of armed workers tried to restore order in the streets and prevent looting. In many places, including the area around our hotel, workers' patrols were posted....

One member of our hotel staff, a middle-aged man with grey hair, told us: "Our workers cannot have had a hand in this looting and rioting. It is fascism raising its head." And that is what it was. The counter-revolutionary underground was in action in Budapest. Fascist reactionary elements had arrived there from abroad. The hostile venture was gathering momentum and the Hungarian Government asked the USSR Government for aid. In response to this request Soviet military units stationed in Hungary under the Warsaw Treaty entered Budapest to help to restore order. The overwhelming majority of Hungarians welcomed this move in the hope that life in the city would quickly return to normal. I myself saw in one street how the people were welcoming the Soviet tanks.

### Thankful for the Tanks

One Hungarian, a member of the hotel staff, described the following incident to us. Firemen-volunteers, absolutely unarmed, were putting out a fire in one of the public buildings. Suddenly, from a small house opposite, shots were fired by fascist louts who opened fire on the unarmed firemen. Several of them fell. Our tank was stationed in the street. The tankmen immediately aimed their gun at the house where the bandits were entrenched. This was sufficient to make them run into a side street. Several firemen ran up to the tank and shook hands with the tankmen. This episode gives a good testimony of the attitude of the Hungarians towards the Soviet troops. However, reaction did not cease its activities. When we walked along some of the streets we saw that the walls of houses were thickly covered with counter-revolutionary posters....

### White Terror

When Soviet troops began withdrawing from Budapest an unbridled White Terror started in the Hungarian capital. We Soviet tourists recall this time with horror. It is difficult to describe the chaos which reigned in the city where public buildings were destroyed, shops looted, and where crowds of armed bandits, obviously fascists, walked along the streets committing bestial murders in broad daylight. I shall never forget what I saw with my own eyes. I think it was on 30 or 31 October. A man in a sports suit walked along the Lenin Boulevard. He might have been one of those who tried to restore order in the city. Several armed ruffians wearing counter-revolutionary tricolours ran up to him. A horrible inhuman cry was heard. A whole crowd of bandits appeared from somewhere. I was unable to see what they were doing with their victim, but in a few minutes he was hanging on a nearby tree with an eye gouged out and his face slashed with knives.

Some time ago I read how the fascists in Germany burnt progressive literature on bonfires. We saw similar things....A group of some hooligans looted and set fire to the House of Books. Thousands and thousands of books were smouldering in the muddy street. We were there, witnesses of this barbarity. The works of Chekhov, Shakespeare, Tolstoi, Pushkin, and other famous authors were lying in the mud, black smoke rising. We saw an old man who lifted a few books, then carefully wiped the mud with his sleeve, pressed them to his breast and walked slowly away. Many people did the same.

---

### Reactionary Scum

The reactionary and counter-revolutionary forces attached themselves to this mass movement and gradually pushed themselves to the forefront. Their purpose was not rectification of mistakes, but the overthrow of the people's democratic system and workers' government....

It was these gentry, with their professional murder techniques, that set streams of blood flowing in the streets of Budapest and other cities. It was this reactionary scum, men who had lost all vestiges of humanity, that destroyed buildings, set fire to shops and factories, smashed up museums and theatres.

*New Times*, no. 47, 1956.

---

In the Hotel "Peace" the atmosphere in those days was extremely tense. The counter-revolutionaries tore the red star from the front of the hotel and trod it underfoot on the pavement. We were told that the Hotel "Peace" from now on would be called Hotel "Britannia." The person who told us about it looked around and added quietly: "It doesn't matter. It will only be temporary."

### Hungarian Friendliness

More than once we were witnesses of acts which manifested the friendly attitude of the Hungarians towards the Soviet people. This friendly attitude was felt by us Soviet people, when we were leaving Budapest....In small groups of two or three people we made our way along the devastated streets towards the Danube in order to board a Red Cross steamer. We were accompanied by a worker ...a young girl. She led us from one cross-road to another, fearlessly seeking the safest way. At the pier we heartily embraced her. She said: "Someone in the West wants us to pull their chestnuts out of the fire. Don't believe them, dear friends. We Hungarians are for socialism and we are with you."

*"We have the possibility of taking into our own hands a common cause,...socialism, and giving it a shape which will better correspond to...the relatively good opinion we once had of ourselves."*

# Reforming Czech Socialism Will Restore National Honor

Ludvík Vaculík

Ludvík Vaculík is a novelist whose speech at a Czech Writers' Congress criticizing Czech Communists proved a harbinger of the liberalizing period which followed President Antonin Novotny's ouster in December 1967. The new Communist leader, Alexander Dubcek, was a reformer who abolished press censorship. Vaculík published "2,000 Words to Workers, Farmers, Scientists, Artists, and Everyone" in a June issue of *Literární listy*, a Czech literary and political weekly. In the following viewpoint, which is an excerpt from "2,000 Words," Mr. Vaculík outlines the mistakes Czech Communists made and advocates limiting their power in an effort to restore Czechoslovakia's national honor.

As you read, consider the following questions:

1. In what ways did the Czech Communist party threaten national honor, according to Mr. Vaculík?
2. Why does the author believe reformers have to work with the Communists?

Ludvík Vaculík, "2,000 Words to Workers, Farmers, Scientists, Artists, and Everyone," *Literární listy*, June 27, 1968.

The life of our nation was first threatened by the war. Then followed another bad time with events which threatened the nation's spiritual health and character. The majority of the nation hopefully accepted the program of socialism. Its direction got into the hands of the wrong people, however. It would not have mattered so much that they did not have sufficient experience as statesmen, practical knowledge, or philosophical education, if they had at least possessed more common sense and decency, if they had been able to listen to the opinion of others, and if they had allowed themselves to be gradually replaced by more capable people.

The Communist party, which after the war possessed the great trust of the people, gradually exchanged this trust for offices, until it had all the offices and nothing else. We must put it this way; those Communists among us know it to be so, and their disappointment over the results is as great as the disappointment of the others. The leadership's incorrect line turned the party from a political party and ideological alliance into a power organization which became very attractive to egotists avid for rule, calculating cowards, and people with bad consciences. Their influx into the party affected its nature and its conduct. Its internal organization was such that honest people who could have magnified it to keep up with the modern world could not wield any influence without shameful accidents. Many Communists fought this decline, but they did not succeed in preventing what happened.

## National Character Threatened

The situation in the Communist party was the pattern and cause of a similar situation in the state. Because the party became linked with the state it lost the advantage of keeping its distance from executive power. There was no criticism of the activity of the state and economic organizations. Parliament forgot how to proceed; the government forgot how to rule and the directors how to direct. Elections had no significance and the laws lost their weight. We could not trust our representatives in any committee, and even if we did, we could not ask them to do anything because they could accomplish nothing. What was still worse was that we had almost lost our trust in one another. Personal and collective honor declined. Honesty led nowhere, and there was no appreciation for ability. Therefore, most people lost interest in public affairs; they were concerned only with themselves and with money. Moreover, as a result of these bad conditions now one cannot even rely on the money. Relations among people were spoiled, joy in one's work lost. To sum up, the country reached a point where its spiritual health and character were threatened.

We are all responsible for the present state of affairs, and the Communists among us are more responsible than others. The main responsibility, however, rests with those who were component parts or instruments of uncontrolled power. It was the power of a tenacious group spread, with the help of the party apparatus, everywhere from Prague to each district and community. The apparatus decided what one might or might not do; it directed the cooperatives for the cooperative members, the factories for the workers, and the national committees for the citizens. No organization actually belonged to its members, not even the Communist organization.

## Will of the Workers

The main guilt and the greatest deception perpetrated by these rulers was that they presented their arbitrary rule as the will of the workers. If we were willing to believe this deception, we would now have to blame the workers for the decline of our economy, for the crimes against innocent people, for the introduction of censorship which made it impossible for all this to be written about. The workers were to blame for the mistaken investments, for the losses in trade, for the shortage of apartments. Naturally, no sensible person believes in such guilt on the part of the workers. We all know and, in particular, each worker knows that in practice the workers did not decide anything. It was someone else who controlled the workers' representatives' vote. While many workers thought that they ruled, the rule was executed in their name by a specially educated group of officials of the party and state apparatus. In effect, they took the place of the overthrown class and themselves became the new authority.

MELODIE BUDOU OVŠEM SPECIFICKY NAŠE!

Hadík

"The melody, of course, will be our own."

*Literární listy*, No. 10, May 2, 1968.

For the sake of justice, we must say that some of them long ago realized this bad game of history. We can recognize them now by the fact that they are redressing wrongs, correcting mistakes, returning decision-making power to the membership and the citizens, and limiting the authority and numbers of *apparatchiks*. They are with us against the obsolete views in the party membership. But many officials are still opposing change, and they still carry weight! They still hold instruments of power, especially in the districts and in the communities, where they may use these instruments secretly and unimpeachably.

From the beginning of the current year, we have been taking part in a revival process of democratization. That it began in the Communist party must be acknowledged. Even people among us outside the party who until recently expected no good to come from us recognize this fact. We must add, however, that this process could not begin elsewhere. After a full twenty years, only the Communists could live something like a political life; only Communist criticism was in a position to see things as they really were; only the opposition within the Communist party had the privilege of being in contact with the enemy. The initiative and efforts of the democratic Communists therefore is only an installment in the repayment of the debt the entire party has incurred with the people outside the party, whom it kept in a position without equal rights. Therefore, no gratitude is due the Communist party, although it should probably be acknowledged that it is honestly striving to use this last opportunity to save its own and the nation's honor.

## Truth's Endurance

The revival process is not contributing any very new things. It is producing ideas and suggestions many of which are older than the errors of our socialism and others of which emerged under the surface of visible events. They should have been expressed long ago; however, they were suppressed. Let us not cherish the illusion that these ideas are now victorious because they wield the force of truth. Their victory was decided rather by the weakness of the old leadership which, obviously, first had to be weakened by a rule of twenty years in which no one hampered it. Obviously, all the defective elements hidden in the very foundations and ideology of this system had to mature before they gained their full form.

Therefore, let us not overestimate the significance of criticism from the ranks of writers and students. The source of social change is the economy. The right word carries significance only if it is spoken under conditions which have already been duly prepared. By duly prepared conditions in our country, unfortunately, we must understand our general poverty and the complete disintegration of the old system of rule, in which politicians of a certain type calmly and peacefully compromised themselves at our expense. Thus, truth is not victorious; truth simply remains when everything else goes to pot! There is no cause for a national celebration of victory; there is merely cause for new hope.

We turn to you in this moment of hope, which, however, is still threatened. It took several months for many of us to believe that we could speak out, and many still do not yet believe it. Nevertheless, we *have* spoken out, and such a great number of things have been revealed that somehow we must complete our aim of humanizing this regime. Otherwise, the revenge of the old forces will be cruel. We turn mainly to those who have so far only waited. The time which will be decisive for many years....

## Drawing Our Own Conclusions

Let us renounce the impossible demand that someone higher up must always give us the only possible interpretation of things, one simple conclusion. Each of us will have to be responsible for drawing his own conclusions. Commonly agreed-upon conclusions can be reached only by discussion, and this requires the freedom of expression which actually is our only democratic achievement of the current year.

In the coming days we will have to display our own personal initiative and determination.

### Source of Power

We ourselves have done nothing to cause the five allies to doubt our loyalty to proletarian internationalism and to all the obligations which we have taken upon ourselves, nothing that could motivate the commentator of *Krasnaya zvezda* to offer us the "help" of the Soviet army to assist us in settling our internal affairs. Our only sin—one, it seems, which is difficult to forgive—is our desire to rid socialism of all its former distortions, to return to it its humane content and its liberating mission, to cleanse the Communist party of bureaucratic-political procedures, to respect our own national tradition, and to fulfill the words of the constitution which says that the only source of power in this state is the people. *Our* people, *our* two nations, in *our* independent and sovereign state.

Ludvík Svoboda, *Obrana lidu*, July 27, 1968.

Above all, we will oppose the view, should it arise, that it is possible to conduct some sort of democratic revival without the Communists or possibly against them. This would be both unjust and unreasonable. The Communists have well-structured organizations, and we should support the progressive wing within them. They have experienced officials and, last but not least, they also have in their hands the decisive levers and buttons. Their action program has been submitted to the public; it is a program for the initial adjustment of the greatest inequalities, and no one else has any similarly concrete program. We must demand that local action programs be submitted to the public in each district and each community. By doing so, we shall have suddenly taken very ordinary and long-expected correct steps. The Czechoslovak Communist Party is preparing for the congress which will elect a new Central Committee. Let us demand that it be better than the current one. If the Communist Party now says that in the future it wants to base its leading position on the citizens' confidence and not on force, let us believe it as long as we can believe in the people whom it is now sending as delegates to the district and regional conferences....

If at this time we cannot expect more from the present central political organs, we must achieve more in the districts and communities. Let us demand the resignation of people who have misused their power, who have damaged public property, or who have acted dishonestly or brutally. We must find ways and means to induce them to resign, for instance, through public criticism, resolutions, demonstrations, demonstration work brigades, collection drives for gifts to them when they retire, strikes, and boycotts of their doors. However, we must reject methods which are illegitimate, improper, or coarse since they might use them to influence Alexander Dubcek.

We must so generally decry the writing of insulting letters that any letter of this kind which they may yet receive could be considered a letter they had sent to themselves. Let us revive the activity of the National Front. Let us demand public meetings of the national committees. To deal with questions which no one wants to know anything about let us set up special citizens' committees and commissions. It is simple: a few people convene, they elect a chairman, keep regular minutes, publish their finding, demand a solution, and do not let themselves be intimidated.

## Defending the Reforms

Let us turn the district and local press, which has degenerated to a mouthpiece of official views, into a platform of all the positive political forces. Let us demand the establishment of editorial councils composed of representatives of the National Front, or let us found newspapers. Let us establish committees for the defense of the freedom of expression. Let us organize our own monitoring service at meetings. If we hear strange news, let us check on it, let us send delegations to the people concerned, and nail their replies to the gates if need be. Let us support the security organs when they persecute genuine criminal activity. We do not mean to cause anarchy and a state of general insecurity. Let us avoid disputes among neighbors. Let us renounce spitefulness in political affairs. Let us reveal informers....

The recent great apprehension results from the possibility that foreign forces may interfere with our internal development.

Faced with all these superior forces the only thing we can do is decently hold our own and not start anything. We can assure our government that we will back it—with weapons if necessary—as long as it does what we give it the mandate to do, and we can assure our allies that we will observe our alliance, friendship, and trade agreements. Excited reproaches and ungrounded suspicions must necessarily make the position of our government more difficult and cannot be of any help to us. At any rate, we can ensure equal relations only by improving our internal conditions and by carrying the process of revival so far that one day at elections we will elect statesmen who will have sufficient courage, honor, and political wisdom to establish and maintain such relations. This, by the way, is a problem of the governments of all small countries in the world.

This spring, as after the war, a great chance has been given us. Again we have the possibility of taking into our own hands a common cause, which has the working title of socialism, and giving it a shape which will better correspond to our once good reputation and the relatively good opinion we once had of ourselves. The spring has now ended and will never return. By winter we will know everything.

*"It is precisely the fraternal collaboration of the socialist countries...that assures...the national interests of each individual country."*

# Reforming Czech Socialism Will Compromise National Interests

I. Alexandrov and P.N. Demichev

The Communist Party of the Soviet Union (CPSU) reacted strongly to Ludvík Vaculík's "2,000 Words." Part I of the following viewpoint is an excerpt from an article I. Alexandrov wrote for *Pravda*, the official Soviet newspaper. He warns that those who signed "2,000 Words" are working against the interests of Czech workers by trying to change Czechoslovakia's socialist system. Part II of the viewpoint is by P.N. Demichev, who, at that time, was a candidate member of the politburo and secretary of the CPSU Central Committee. He argues that imperialists use nationalism to subvert socialism. His article was published in *Kommunist*, the CPSU's journal.

As you read, consider the following questions:

1. According to Mr. Alexandrov, how are those who signed "2,000 Words" trying to strike out "the entire history of Czechoslovakia since 1948"?
2. What distinction does Mr. Demichev draw between national liberation movements and imperialist nationalism?

I. Alexandrov, "Attack on the Socialist Foundations of Czechoslovakia," *Pravda*, July 11, 1968. Translation copyright 1968 by The Current Digest of the Soviet Press, published weekly at Columbus, Ohio. Reprinted by permission of the Digest. P.N. Demichev, "Building of Communism and the Tasks of the Social Sciences," *Kommunist*, July 1968.

# I

Rightist, antisocialist forces continue to mount malicious and fierce attacks against the Communist Party and the socialist system. And many of these subversive actions are conducted openly, with the use of the Czechoslovak press, radio and television.

Not so long ago, for example, four Czechoslovak newspapers— Literarni Listy, Prace, Zemedelske Noviny and Mlada Fronta— simultaneously published a so-called open letter from a group of persons; it was entitled "2,000 Words to Workers, Peasants, Employees, Scientists, People in the Arts, to All Citizens."

The document is a sort of platform representing the forces in Czechoslovakia and abroad that are endeavoring, under the guise of talk about "liberalization," "democratization," etc., to strike out the entire history of Czechoslovakia since 1948 and the socialist achievements of the Czechoslovak working people, to discredit the Czechoslovak Communist Party and its leading role, to undermine the friendship between the Czechoslovak people and the peoples of fraternal socialist states and to pave the way for counterrevolution.

The authors of the document slander the C.C.P. and the socialist system in alleging that the "leadership's erroneous line turned the party from a political party and an ideological alliance into a great-power organization"; that "Parliament has forgotten how to discuss problems, the government how to govern, and the directors how to direct"; that "not a single organization actually belonged to its members, not even the Communist organization"; and that "the Communist Party deserves no gratitude." In essence the statement praises bourgeois Czechoslovakia and does not conceal its sympathies for the capitalist system.

## Defending Czech Interests

Moreover, in attempting to activate antisocialist elements, the authors of the appeal and those who back them declare that the "ensuing period will be decisive for many years to come" and demand the right to present "their own decisions." They call for the use of such means as demonstrations, strikes and boycotts in order to get rid of party personnel and leaders, devoted to the cause of socialism, who do not suit them. They demand the "establishment of their own civic committees and commissions" in the localities, i.e., the seizure of power. They promise to act "with arms in hand" in favor of the leadership to which they will give their "mandate."

"The 2,000 Words," despite hypocritical phrases about "defending" the interests of the Czechoslovak people, leaves no doubt as to the authors' real objectives. They speak on behalf of the rightest, antisocialist forces in the country that are attacking the C.C.P. and the working class. Every day brings new facts to confirm that these forces are by no means concerned with correcting errors or with further developing Czechoslovakia along the road of socialism, but have taken the course of overthrowing the existing system and restoring capitalism. They do not say this openly; more often than not, they cover up their true objectives with phrases about "democratization" and declare their support for socialism. But in actual fact they are seeking to undermine the very foundations of the socialist state.

Such tactics are not new. They were resorted to by the counter-revolutionary elements in Hungary that in 1956 sought to undermine the socialist achievements of the Hungarian people. Now, 12 years later, the tactics of those who would like to undermine the foundations of socialism in Czechoslovakia are even more subtle and insidious. And the Czechoslovak working people, as well as all who hold dear the achievements of socialism, cannot fail to see the danger concealed behind the incitive, provocational activity urged by "The 2,000 Words."

---

## Bourgeois Propaganda

Having lost hope of gaining the upper hand over socialism by frontal attack, by carrying out the so-called strategy of rolling back communism, imperialists have not renounced their aims but have only changed their methods....

They rely most on revisionist, nationalist, and politically immature elements. Bourgeois propaganda highly lauds elements of this kind, praises them, and represents them as heroes. Anti-Communist ideologists do not conceal that the aim of all this advertising is to encourage activity which might lead toward "erosion" of socialism, permit its decomposition from within, and finally lead to restoration of capitalism in socialist countries. There is no doubt that this move by imperialism will be defeated just like all the previous ones. The Soviet people and the peoples of other socialist countries have joined their fates firmly and forever with socialism and communism; they will allow no one to divert them from this road.

V.V. Grishin, *Pravda*, April 23, 1968.

---

The healthy forces in the party and in the country view this document as an overt attack on the socialist system, on the C.C.P.'s guiding role and on Czechoslovakia's friendship with the Soviet Union and other socialist countries....

## Condemning Counterrevolution

The publication of "The 2,000 Words" aroused much reaction in the country. The majority of the C.C.P. party organizations, as well as Communists who spoke at recent district conferences, condemned this counterrevolutionary platform. The Czechoslovak government and the National Front also spoke of it in negative terms.

At the National Assembly session, Deputy S. Kodaj justifiably called "The 2,000 Words" a "call for counterrevolution." Public organizations and the collectives of enterprises and institutions have also expressed sharp criticism.

At the same time as the party conferences and groups of working people, guided by the interests of strengthening socialism in the country and consolidating the Czechoslovak people's fraternal friendship with the peoples of the Soviet Union and other socialist countries, are rebuffing the new attack on Czechoslovakia's socialist foundations; some press and information organs in Czechoslovakia have taken a "special" position. The newspapers Prace, Zemedelske Noviny and Mlada Fronta and Prague radio and television are endeavoring to influence public opinion toward supporting "The 2,000 Words." In doing this they attempt to make it seem as if they speak on behalf of the people.

Judging from the Czechoslovak press, some reactionary journalists and writers have been expressing support for this position. These are the same people who have more than once called for putting an end to the C.C.P.'s guiding role and for returning to a "democracy" that would in fact mean the restoration of capitalism. It is precisely these people who are defending the "2,000 Words" statement, who are seeking to present it as the last word of some sort of unprecedented "socialist democracy" and who are quick to label as "conservatives" those who speak out against the counterrevolutionary statement "2,000 Words."

## Ambiguous Statements

Unfortunately, some Czechoslovak leaders have made ambiguous statements attempting to minimize the danger of the "2,000 Words" statement and declaring that the fact of its promulgation "need not be dramatized."

Rightist forces hostile to socialism hastened to exploit the fact that some people found it necessary both to conceal the incitive character of the document and to gloss over the criticism by the Czechoslovak working people. In the last few days these forces, with the help of certain press organs, have been giving wide publicity to "The 2,000 Words."

It has now become more obvious than ever that the appearance of "The 2,000 Words" is not an isolated phenomenon, but evidence of the increasing activity in Czechoslovakia of rightist and overtly counterrevolutionary forces obviously linked with imperialist reaction. They have gone on to make fierce attacks against the foundations of socialist statehood. Evidently, forces hostile to the Czechoslovak people are hastening to take advantage of the unstable situation in the country in order to achieve their counterrevolutionary goals. The support that these forces have found among imperialists in the West is playing a considerable role in all this, as can be distinctly seen in connection with the publication of "The 2,000 Words."

# II

If one were to define briefly the essence of the global political strategy of the imperialist bourgeoisie, it would consist of the following: the use of all ways and means to undermine the positions of socialism, weaken its influences and authority, and inflict losses on it. For these purposes the bourgeoisie is undertaking tremendous efforts to completely utilize...the nationalistic tendencies of the revisionists of various colorations; turning socialist countries against one another, and especially against the Soviet Union—the embodiment of the power and unity of the entire worldwide system of socialism; and attempting to force a wedge between the socialist countries and the worldwide Communist movement on the one hand and the national liberation movement on the other.

---

### Apple of Our Eye

We shall guard as the apple of our eye our fraternal ties of alliance and friendship with the Soviet Union, its people, the peoples of all the countries in the world socialist commonwealth and with all the forces of peace, democracy, progress and socialism—these are the values that guarantee us our autonomy, independence and national and state sovereignty, without which we would again be faced with the threat of a new Munich and with those who organized it in 1938. Czechoslovakia can develop only as a socialist country and as an inseparable component of the socialist commonwealth; its strength and stability create the bases for the future prospects of the international revolutionary movement; any weakening and disruption of the socialist camp would cause a harm difficult to imagine to the cause of revolutionary progress and socialism in the world.

Members of CCP Central Committee and CSR Government and National Assembly, *Pravda*, August 22, 1968.

---

A very important peculiarity of the tactics of imperialism at the present stage consists of the fact that it is counting on undermining the socialist countries from within. The imperialist bourgeoisie understands that an open attack upon socialism at the present time is too risky. Therefore, instead of open summonses to overthrow the authority of the working class, to liquidate socialism, and to restore capitalist orders, the opponents of the new system, more and more frequently, are given the advice to "modernize" socialism, speak out against the leading role of the Communist party, and effect a gradual substitution of socialist democracy by bourgeois-parliamentarian democracy. With that aim, there has been a popularization of the slogan for a kind of "liberalization" of socialism and the creation of equal opportunities for various, including nonsocialist, parties; and there has been a propagandizing of a non-class interpretation of freedom and humanitarianism.

It is necessary to understand correctly the new tactic of imperialist reaction, which is changing, more and more frequently, from frontal attacks on socialism to a tactic of maneuvering, to a search for circuitous routes, and it is necessary to know how to combat it....

## Revisionist Nationalism

The imperialist bourgeoisie combine direct attacks upon socialism and the worldwide Communist movement with attempts to cause the "erosion" of Marxism. They praise to the skies the modern revisionists who, under the guise of combating dogmatism and eliminating the "deformation" of Marxism, are attacking the fundamental principles of scientific communism, and primarily the theory concerning the universal historical role of the working class and the dictatorship of the proletariat, and concerning the party and the party monopoly of ideology....

A characteristic feature of the revisionism of our day consists of the fact that in many instances, not only on the basis of substance, but also on the basis of their argumentation and the formulation of their initial policy premises, the "leftists" not only stand right alongside the rightists, but frequently are simply indistinguishable from them. For example, anti-Sovietism, slander directed against the Soviet Union and the CPSU, constitute the common platform of all the revisionists and unite them with professional anti-Communists.

Nationalism is taking greater and greater form as a serious danger. As a rule, nationalism, intertwining with revisionist tendencies of all trends, constitutes the common feature that is typical of opportunistic conceptions that replace Marxism-Leninism as an international theory by its "national" versions....

Our enemies cast aspersions on the socialist state, attempting to discredit and undermine the leading role of the Communist party in the system of the political organization of the socialist society, to belittle the importance and value of the civil and political rights of man under socialism, and to besmirch the Soviet social and state system. They attempt to poison the consciousness of the workers with counterrevolutionary ideas of "democracy without Communists," of "pure" democracy, and "absolute freedom."

Historical experience has shown that expatiations concerning democracy and "liberalization" are used by counterrevolutions as a smoke screen for attempts to liquidate the conquests of socialism and socialist democracy. We can recall how, during the Hungarian events of 1956, it was under those slogans that counterrevolution meted out bloody drumhead justice to Communists.

Therefore, it is necessary to give a prompt and decisive rebuff to all attempts by imperialist apologists to slander the socialist state and socialist democracy; it is necessary to carry the truth about our social and state system to the workers of other countries. At the same time we must speak out against the erroneous understanding of the nature of democratic freedoms under socialism.

The gage of real democratism is not abstract freedom for all—not only for friends, but also for enemies of socialism. The main thing in socialist democracy is the complete freedom of the individual from exploitation, the growth of the activity and consciousness of the masses, who, by their activity, infuse new blood into all the democratic establishments and institutions....

National problems are presently the object of especially acute ideological warfare. Nationalism is emerging as one of the most dangerous weapons of the imperialists for causing a schism in the ranks of the workers' liberation movement.

In our time, numerous liberation movements of oppressed peoples are developing under the banner of nationalism. In this form one finds expressions of the progressive desires of broad segments of the people which oppose the reactionary nationalism of the imperialist bourgeoisie. But the nationalism of the democratic liberation movements reveals also its narrowness, it can, under certain circumstances turn into feeble reactionary impulses with regard to other peoples, and can also infect some of the Communists with a narrow nationalistic approach.

## Socialist Internationalism

It should be taken into consideration that the development of the so-called "third world" has been the economic, political, and ideological influence not only of the Soviet Union and the worldwide socialist system, but also of imperialism, with all its economic might, and well-developed apparatus for spreading propaganda, including the propaganda of nationalist ideas....

At the basis of proletarian, socialist internationalism lies the acknowledgement not only of the equal rights of nations, but also the unity of international and national interests. That was repeatedly indicated by V. I. Lenin. It has been proven by life that it is precisely the fraternal collaboration of the socialist countries on the basis of the principles of proletarian internationalism that assures, and most solidly guarantees, the national interests of each individual country.

*"There remains in Japan a...potentially dangerous political group whose goal is remilitarization.... [and whose philosophy] is ultra-nationalist."*

# Japanese Nationalism Remains a Danger

Henry Scott Stokes

Japan is still humiliated by its defeat in World War II and the American occupation that followed, according to Henry Scott Stokes, the author of the following viewpoint. Mr. Stokes writes about Yukio Mishima, a right-wing, nationalist author who committed *seppuku*, ritual public suicide, in 1970. Mishima despaired over modern Japan's acceptance of Western values. He yearned for Japan's samurai era, a time when warlords ruled and Westerners were excluded. Mr. Stokes has written *The Life and Death of Yukio Mishima* and is a contributing editor at *Harper's*.

As you read, consider the following questions:

1. How has the commercialism associated with capitalism violated Japan's cultural values in the opinion of the author?
2. What does the author conclude is "the true meaning" of Mishima's suicide?
3. Who were Mishima's powerful allies, according to Mr. Stokes, and why did they support him?
4. How does the author believe that Japan's view of suicide differs from the West's view?

Literature has fallen into disrepute in Japan of late. Instead of dreaming of writing novels, today's young Japanese dream of writing software programs. But the Japanese once venerated their great novelists as moral spokesmen. The leading novelists of the 1960s—Kobo Abe, Kenzaburo Oe, Shusaku Endo—were the uncrowned kings of the Japanese intellectual world. Without a doubt, Yukio Mishima was the most singular member of this talented company. A popular and prolific writer, Mishima was also a self-avowed homosexual with a wife and two children, a trenchant critic, a tough-guy movie actor, a muscular sportsman, and an emperor-worshipping right-wing political activist who, in his spare time, commanded a private army. When the *New York Times Magazine* featured him on its cover in 1970, it described him as "the Renaissance man of Japan."...It was from Yukio's death—his sensational public suicide by disembowelment on November 25, 1970—that I at last learned the sobering truth about postwar Japan....

## Bitter Loss of Face

Japan is still deeply traumatized by its unconditional surrender to the Allies. At the end of World War II, the Japanese, heirs to a military tradition that stretches back eight centuries, found themselves under the thumb of a foreign power for the first time in more than 2,000 years of recorded history; they were forced to abandon an ancient tradition of martial valor and to accept an American-drafted constitution in which "the Japanese people forever renounce war as a sovereign right of the nation and the threat or the use of force as a means of settling international disputes." Viewed against the backdrop of so bitter a loss of face, the postwar prosperity of the Japanese is a mere triviality. They see their vast wealth as minimal compensation for the hideous humiliation of the American occupation, which, with military bases in every strategic corner of the Japanese archipelago, continues to this day.

The Japanese have built one of the richest and most productive nations on earth. But the cost has been high: they have had to set aside their ancient culture and shatter their country's ecology. There is no restoring the primeval forests and white sand beaches that have been taken over by businessmen's golf courses and giant concrete tetrapods. To the average American, unsightly highways are at worst a minor scenic annoyance; to the Japanese, whose aesthetic tendencies permeate every aspect of day-to-day life, the cost of capitalism has necessarily been agonizing. And prosperity has brought more than barren beaches. The country's leading artists have been pushed to the edge of an abyss of apathy and paralysis....

For Yukio, Japan was a victim of American imperialism; he was convinced that the Japanese had abandoned their own values and been culturally colonized by America. Not that he had a solution, a policy. No, all Yukio really wanted was to see the barbarians driven back into the sea. And he didn't particularly care how the job was to be done. At the end he despised Western culture; most of all, he rejected Western humanist ideals, which he thought were a poisonous threat to the Japanese spirit. In his novel *Runaway Horses*, Yukio wrote:

> As Isao watched he realized that before one could attack with one's whole being like Sawa, there were many rivers to be leaped over. And one clouded stream that never ran dry was that choked with the scum of humanism, the poison spewed out by the factory at its headwaters. There it was: its lights burning brilliantly as it worked even through the night—the factory of Western European ideals. The pollution from that factory degraded the exalted fervor to kill....

Isao, a thirties terrorist, Mishima's alter ego, and the hero of the book, is here taking a lesson from Sawa on how to stab a man to death. His target is an aging capitalist—a symbol of the bourgeois West.

═══════════════════════════════════════

## Courageous Losers

For all [Mishima's] own worldly success, the people he most admired were men like Oshio Heihachiro (the perfervid Police Inspector who stabbed himself to death after the collapse of his uprising in 1837), the members of the League of the Divine Wind who were slaughtered in the rebellion of 1876, and the young suicide pilots who died in the war against America. This spontaneous sympathy with the courageous loser was no personal quirk of Mishima's but has deep roots among the Japanese, who since ancient times have recognized a special nobility in the sincere, unsuccessful sacrifice....

Ever since the end of the Pacific war, he wrote, the Japanese people have been determined to "play it safe," attaching overwhelming importance to security and material ease and ignoring what is unique and most precious in their country's heritage. In consequence their bodies go on living longer than before but their spirits die an early death.

Ivan Morris, *The Nobility of Failure: Tragic Heroes in the History of Japan*, 1975.

═══════════════════════════════════════

It is against this background that the true meaning of Yukio Mishima's suicide must be sought. Westerners, who have no conception of suicide as an honorable act sanctioned by tradition, find it hard to grasp the implications of Mishima's death; it is as if Ernest Hemingway had chosen to end his suffering with one last grand gesture at high noon in the *plaza de toros*, rather than by blowing off his head in the privacy of his own home. But Mishima's suicide was more than a gesture. It was a bloody metaphor for the passion of postwar Japan, a metaphor written not with brush and ink but with a samurai's short sword driven into the belly of a great novelist. And it left a deep wound in the collective consciousness of Japan: the Japanese are not sure whether to praise Mishima or curse him; he is, as a friend of mine said recently, a peculiarly "inconvenient" person.

## Reviving National Pride

Yukio Mishima must have known that the prominent right-wing politicians who had so stealthily backed him would instantly disavow him on hearing of his suicide. But he paid them no heed, fully committed as he was to a cause that the politicians of his day were not prepared to discuss openly: the cause of reviving the national pride and remilitarizing Japan....

[Alvin] Toffler, in his book *Previews and Premises*,...acknowledged the immense significance of Yukio's death—that fleeting glimpse into the cauldron of anti-Americanism that seethes at the center of Japanese life.

> The Mishima incident a decade or so ago ought to remind Washington that there remains in Japan a tiny, yet virulent and potentially dangerous, political group whose goal is remilitarization. Every time Washington twists Japan's arm to spend more on warplanes or to increase the size of its navy to help patrol the Pacific sea lanes, it inadvertently lends support to this group of extremists—which, as a matter of fact, is ultra-nationalist and hence anti-American....The result is a rising resentment that could easily explode if trade and economic pressures worsen.

One wonders whether Toffler would modify these remarks if he knew that the "tiny yet virulent group" numbers among its members two Japanese prime ministers.

Imagine the following scenario: Norman Mailer, having definitively lost interest in the novel as a viable art form, goes on television and proclaims himself to be a neo-Nazi. He organizes a small group of eccentric right-wing college students into a private army which he proposes to use to help the police quell anti-apartheid protests at various universities. Caspar Weinberger, seeking to further his political ambitions, gives Mailer permission to train his army at Fort Benning. And Ronald Reagan diverts from a slush fund the cash necessary to underwrite Mailer's activities.

## Powerful Allies

In America, such a scenario would be absurd on the face of it; in Japan, though such things do not happen every day, something very similar did happen to Yukio Mishima. Early in 1968, around the time I first came to know him, Yukio decided to organize what he called "the world's smallest and most spiritual army." Yukio's private army, known as the Tatenokai—Japanese for Shield

Society—consisted of about seventy students. Many of them were drawn from sports clubs at Tokyo universities; most of them were politically well to the right. They trained at a boot camp on Mount Fuji, where, in the spring of 1969, I witnessed an all-day exercise in which regular officers from the Japanese Self-Defense Forces were giving the orders....

## Defense Buildup

Japan, the country with the famous no-war constitution, limits defense spending to 1 percent of the gross national product. Nonetheless, it is conducting a sustained buildup that has made it the world's eighth largest defense spender after France....

Japan's defense buildup has attracted wide international attention under Nakasone's outward-looking government. But, in fact, it has been in motion with hardly a pause since the day the forces were commissioned in 1954. Growth rates are larger than those of the United States.

John Burgess, *Washington Post National Weekly Edition*, August 26, 1985.

For all his candor, Yukio never shared with me the full story of the Tatenokai; I discovered it on my own after his death. It turned out that he had two very powerful allies in high places: Eisaku Sato, prime minister of Japan from 1964 to 1972, and Yasuhiro Nakasone, who was defense minister at the time of Mishima's death and who is now prime minister. Sato underwrote the activities of the Tatenokai with funds raised by right-wing Japanese businessmen; Nakasone made it possible for Yukio to train his army on Mount Fuji. (To date, no Japanese newspaper has printed anything about the Mishima-Nakasone-Sato connection, though its existence is widely known among Japanese journalists.)

## Political Ties

The truth about Yukio's ties to the Japanese right will probably not be known for decades. But I do not doubt that what persuaded the two prime ministers to back him was the fact that he was the only respected intellectual of his generation who openly espoused right-wing ideals and the old slogans of emperor worship. The leaders of the ruling party believed that it was losing its broad base of public support and needed to increase its following among the young. At which point appeared the obliging Mishima, shouting his anachronistic slogans and posturing on the battlements. He must immediately have struck Sato and Nakasone as an ally in the battle for public opinion. In such a fashion was the unholy alliance between Yukio and the politicians sealed....

It is tempting to speculate on why Sato and Nakasone ever gave their wholehearted support to Mishima. It is clear that these lesser men wanted to see Japanese pride restored. They wanted the constitution revised. (It is known that one of Nakasone's principal "spiritual advisers" is a grizzled, bullet-headed old man named Yotsumoto—a survivor of the ill-fated 1936 coup who is regarded as a kind of permanent portable shrine by the extreme right in Japan.) They wanted the military legalized. They wanted Article IX repealed. They wanted the forces that protect Japan to be Japanese, not American. Their problem was that the Japanese public did not—and does not—trust the Japanese military. Memories of the war die hard. The Japanese remember, for example, the horrors of Unit 731 in Manchuria, which conducted "medical" experiments on living Chinese that rank with anything Mengele did at Auschwitz. Such unhappy memories are kept out of textbooks by the mandarins of the Education Ministry. But the Japanese people still remember.

How, then, were "conservatives" like Sato and Nakasone to deal with the grass-roots resistance to rearmament? This was the major problem facing the Japanese right two decades ago, and Sato and Nakasone must have seen in Mishima a way to mobilize the feelings of a suspicious public. In the short run, the gamble failed ignominiously; the fiasco of Mishima's suicide probably set back the crusade for rearmament by at least a decade. But this setback will surely be temporary....

We are likely to witness a gradual change in Japan's military posture while efforts to revise the "peace constitution" gather steam. But massive rearmament, public opinion notwithstanding, is *almost* inevitable. Prime Minister Nakasone is moving to eliminate the ceiling on defense spending, which has been in effect since 1976; parliament, which voted the ceiling, now appears ready to reverse its decision. If one extrapolates from current trends, the Japan of twenty years hence could well be one of the most militarily powerful nations in the world. And I find that a deeply unsettling prospect.

### Tradition of Self-Destruction

Why? Because of the hallowed tradition of self-destruction which is at the heart of Japanese culture and history. One sees it in the ritual of harakiri, which dates back to the thirteenth century; one sees it in the decision to attack Pearl Harbor, a decision that makes Hitler's move to invade the Soviet Union in 1941 seem meticulously considered by comparison. And one sees it in the case of Yukio Mishima: a world-famous author in his mid-forties, a man who had just missed receiving the Nobel Prize, by far the best-known Japanese in the West apart from the emperor himself, who chose at the peak of his success to commit suicide in a seemingly futile attempt to galvanize the Japanese will....

In the eyes of a Mishima, worldwide nuclear holocaust—the prospect of which he frankly romanticized in his diaries—might well be the proper aesthetic response to the death of civility implicit in the idea of a commercialized Japan.

Not long ago a friend of mine, the distinguished historian Nobutoshi Hagihara, proposed in his book *Experiencing the Twentieth Century* that the government should hold a referendum on the 1947 constitution, giving the general public its first real opportunity to affirm that the constitution, with its renunciation of force, is more than just the hated product of foreign devils long since dead. This seems to me an essential step. Today, Japan has no strategic forces at all: no nuclear submarines, no aircraft carriers, no nuclear-tipped ICBMs. I do not know what is to come in Japan. But I am sure of this: the world is in enough trouble as it is without adding to its infinite complications the terrifying prospect of a suicidal, nuclear-armed Japan.

*"Since the end of [World War II], Japan has profoundly regretted the ultranationalism and militarism it unleashed, and the untold suffering the war inflicted."*

# Japan Has Renounced Militant Nationalism

Yasuhiro Nakasone

Japanese Prime Minister Yasuhiro Nakasone argues in the following viewpoint that Japan regrets the militant nationalism which led it into World War II. He also notes that although his country renounced ultranationalism following the war, it still respects and draws upon its distinctive cultural traditions. Mr. Nakasone was an officer in the Japanese Navy during World War II and is a former minister of defense. In a speech to the United Nations General Assembly, from which this viewpoint is excerpted, Mr. Nakasone asked all nations to recognize the universal values they share and to renounce selfish nationalist policies.

As you read, consider the following questions:

1. Does Mr. Nakasone see a conflict between Japan's traditions and the values he terms universal?
2. In what way do "selfish national policies" threaten free trade, according to the author?
3. How can political programs reduce national barriers and promote an international, peaceful civilization, according to Mr. Nakasone?

Yasuhiro Nakasone, Address to Commemorative 40th Anniversary Session of the United Nations, UN General Assembly, New York, October 23, 1985.

At the time the United Nations Charter was signed in San Francisco on 26 June 1945, Japan was waging a desperate and lonely war against over 40-odd Allied countries. Since the end of that war, Japan has profoundly regretted the ultranationalism and militarism it unleashed, and the untold suffering the war inflicted upon peoples around the world and, indeed, upon its own people.

In seeking to rebuild their homeland, the Japanese people, while respecting their own distinctive traditions and culture, eagerly embraced the universal and fundamental human values—namely, freedom, democracy and human rights—and formulated a new Constitution based upon these truths.

## Scourge of War

Japan has vowed, to itself and the world, to remain a peaceful State possessing the capability for self-defense only, and never again to become a military power. Having suffered the scourge of war and the atomic bomb, the Japanse people will never again permit the revival of militarism on their soil....

Japan has made the United Nations a central pillar of its foreign policy, and it has sought Japanese peace and prosperity within the broader context of global peace and prosperity.

Our commitment is evident first in our efforts to promote world peace and disarmament, especially to banish nuclear weapons from this earth.

As the only people ever to have experienced the devastation of the atomic bomb, in Hiroshima and Nagasaki, the Japanese people have steadfastly called for the elimination of nuclear weapons. Nuclear energy should be used exclusively for peaceful purposes; it must never again be employed as a means of destruction. The nuclear-weapon States should lend a responsive ear to the world's urgent appeals for the elimination of nuclear weapons....

## Commitment to Global Peace

Japan's commitment to global peace and prosperity is also evident in its efforts to promote free trade and to cooperate with developing countries.

Following the bitter experiences of the 1930s, free trade has been nurtured among nations as a guiding principle for the postwar world economy. Yet, free trade is as fragile as glass; if we do not take care, even the slightest shock may shatter it to bits. Because free trade is premised upon competition, it inevitably inflicts pain on certain industries in every country. Yet if countries fall back on selfish national policies in an effort to avoid this pain, then clearly the entire structure of free trade will collapse.

Like a powerful narcotic, protectionism may induce a feeling of temporary well-being in the industries it is supposed to protect. But protectionism not only saps the vitality of its users, it also begets further protectionism, and ultimately the world economy will lapse into a coma.

We must therefore rededicate ourselves to resisting the lure of protectionism and to preserving and fortifying the free trade system....

## Japan's Moral Duty

Itself a developing country only one hundred years ago, Japan achieved its modernization and industrialization with the support of many advanced countries. We well understand the aspirations and frustrations of developing countries.

Today, it is Japan's turn to help others, and I believe Japan has a moral duty and major international responsibility to use its economic power, technology and experience to assist developing countries in their nation-building and human-resource development efforts.

---

### No Lamenting

Most Japanese either don't want to be reminded about Mishima's suicide or simply don't care. The questions that Mishima tried to force down Japanese throats in 1970 are even less relevant today. Near the end of Mishima's life, Japan was shaken by student rebellion and deepening social schisms. Mishima warned that the money-grubbing of the country's merchant elite would tear Japan apart. On the contrary, prosperity has made Japan less volatile— both more cohesive and more open to pluralistic thought and diverse behavior. Prosperity also has brought new problems: higher rates of divorce, suicide and alcoholism. But with their freer, less tradition-bound lifestyles, few young people lament the loss of their samurai souls.

Tracy Dahlby, *Newsweek*, December 9, 1985.

---

I have long reminded the people of Japan and other industrialized countries that there can be no prosperity for the North without prosperity for the South. I firmly believe this to be true, and I believe Japan has an important global mission to act as a bridge between North and South....

Japan's concern for global peace and prosperity is evident also in its cooperation with peoples throughout the world in the development of culture and civilization.

### Promoting International Exchanges

Culture is the supreme mark of man, and I believe that the goal of politics is to contribute to culture. From this perspective, I have placed special emphasis in domestic politics on education, scholarship, the arts, science and technology, and environment, all of which foster the enrichment of culture. Such efforts are today increasingly important in the international community as well.

International exchanges in science and technology, the arts, sports, scholarship, and other fields provide indispensable support for peace and cultural creativity. We ought to take full advantage of the remarkable advances being made in transportation, communications and information processing, to lower and even remove the walls that separate the peoples of the world. We ought to promote more international exchanges among peoples, giving the fullest respect to the human rights of all peoples, and in this way, build a truly peaceful world civilization. I believe success in maintaining peace depends upon nothing less than mankind's collective conscience and the level of cultural exchange among peoples.

As a nation committed to peace and cultural development,... Japan has cooperated faithfully and vigorously with its activities, providing financial support, information and personnel. We intend to strengthen our support, giving particular attention to such issues as the environment, population and health....

## Ancestral Traditions

We Japanese derive our beliefs and philosophy from traditions handed down by our ancestors over thousands of years, and from later influences of Confucianism and Buddhism. Basic to our philosophy is the concept that man is born by the grace of the great universe. Japanese poets throughout history have expressed this concept in their poems. In this tradition I composed this *haiku* one evening:

| | |
|---|---|
| A-ma-no-ga-wa | Afar and above the dark and endless sky, |
| Wa-ga fu-ru-sa-to ni | the Milky Way runs |
| Na-ga-re-ta-ri | toward the place I come from. |

We Japanese generally believe that the great natural universe is our home, and that all living things should co-exist in harmony with the natural universe. We believe that all living things—humans, animals, trees, grasses—are essentially brothers and sisters.

## Universal Values

I doubt that this philosophy is unique to the Japanese. I believe that better understanding of it could contribute much to the creation of universal values for our international community.

The human potential for creativity is distributed evenly among all peoples in all lands, and all the different religious beliefs and artistic traditions in the world are equally unique and equally valuable. The starting point for world peace is, I believe, a recognition of this diversity of human culture and a humble attitude of mutual appreciation and respect.

If we can all start with this attitude, then I believe all cultures and civilization in the world will progress, and we can create a new and truly harmonious global civilization for all humanity.

# Distinguishing Between Fact and Opinion

This activity is designed to help develop the basic reading and thinking skill of distinguishing between fact and opinion. Consider the following statement as an example: "The Soviet army invaded Hungary on November 4, 1956." This statement is a fact easily verified in any history book. But consider another statement about Hungary and the Soviet Union: "The Soviet Union committed a moral error when it invaded Hungary." This statement suggests a value judgment which is someone's opinion. It is not a fact.

When investigating controversial issues it is important that one be able to distinguish between statements of fact and statements of opinion. It is also important to recognize that not all statements of fact are true. They may appear to be true, but some are based on inaccurate or false information. For this activity, however, we are concerned with understanding the difference between those statements which appear to be factual and those which appear to be based primarily on opinion.

Most of the following statements are taken from the viewpoints in this chapter. Consider each statement carefully. *Mark O for any statement you believe is an opinion or interpretation of facts. Mark F for any statement you believe is a fact.*

If you are doing this activity as a member of a class or group, compare your answers with those of other class or group members. Be able to defend your answers. You may discover that others will come to different conclusions than you. Listening to the reasons others present for their answers may give you valuable insights in distinguishing between fact and opinion.

If you are reading this book alone, ask others if they agree with your answers. You too will find this interaction very valuable.

O = *opinion*
F = *fact*

1. Comrade Imre Nagy speaking over the radio indicated that "a handful of counterrevolutionary instigators staged an armed attack against the regime."

2. We arrived in Hungary on 19 October with other Soviet tourists.

3. The students' demands were legitimate.

4. Soon there were flashes of gunfire and sounds of battle and we saw wrecked and burning buildings in the streets of Budapest.

5. The workers cannot have had a hand in this looting and rioting.

6. The true Hungarians are for socialism.

7. The government formally rejects the view that sees the present popular movement as a counter-revolution.

8. Great opportunities should be provided for our workers, peasants, and students in our purified political life.

9. The government has ordered an immediate cease-fire.

10. Béla Kovács spent eight years in Siberia.

11. The economic salvation of Hungary lies in a mixed economy, combining capitalism, state ownership, and cooperatives.

12. The Hungarian revolution has brought modern history to a turning point.

13. If the Soviets are trying to revert to the old Stalinist days, they will fail even more miserably than before.

14. Four Czechoslovak newspapers published "2,000 Words" simultaneously.

15. The authors of the letter call for demonstrations, strikes, and boycotts to get rid of party personnel and leaders.

16. While the workers thought they ruled the government, the rule was executed in their name by party bureaucrats.

17. We owe no gratitude to the Communist party.

# Bibliography

The following list of books, periodicals, and pamphlets deals with the subject matter of this chapter.

| | |
|---|---|
| Timothy Garton Ash | "The Hungarian Lesson," *The New York Review of Books*, December 5, 1985. |
| John F.N. Bradley | "Prague Spring 1968 in Historical Perspective," *East European Quarterly*, September 1982. |
| Zbigniew Brzezinski | "Japan Should End Free Ride by Devoting Four Percent of GNP to Aid and Defense," *Los Angeles Times*, August 13, 1985. |
| *Defense Monitor* | "The Defense of Japan: Should the Rising Sun Rise Again?" *The Defense Monitor*, vol. 13, no. 1, 1984. |
| Peter Fryer | *Hungarian Tragedy*. London: Dobson Books, Ltd., 1956. |
| Milan Kundera | *The Book of Laughter and Forgetting*, a novel. New York: Alfred A. Knopf, 1981. 1981. |
| Anthony Lewis | "Angry at Success," *The New York Times*, August 12, 1985. |
| Yukio Mishima | *Runaway Horses*, a novel. New York, NY: Alfred A. Knopf, 1973. |
| *New Times* | "Czechoslovakia," no. 35, September 1968. |
| *New Times* | "Hungary," no. 47, November 1956. |
| Josef Skvorecky | "Big Beat Vs. Big Brother," *The New Republic*, December 17, 1984. |
| Lynn Turgeon | "Aren't You Hungary for Market Socialism?" *The Guardian*, January 8, 1986. |
| George Urban | "The People Are Coming!": A Remarkable Political Confession," *Encounter*, September/October 1985. |

# Contemporary Nationalism in the Middle East

# Introduction

Nationalism has clearly shown its power to disrupt human lives in the Middle East. Extremist factions motivated by nationalism attack their opponents, often killing innocent people in the process. Recently, such terrorist actions have directly affected the lives of Americans and Europeans living and traveling abroad who have been caught in hijackings, shootings, bombings and, in some cases, have been held hostage.

This random violence seems scarcely understandable to those who are insulated from Middle East chaos. Many are bewildered by the seemingly sudden and extreme appearance of terrorism in their lives. This final chapter examines contemporary Middle Eastern nationalism in hopes of making more clear to readers how frustrated national ambitions lead many groups to violence.

Rabbi Meir Kahane's nationalism finds its roots in the bitter persecution Jews experienced for centuries throughout the world. Shimon Peres recalls the terrorist tactics Palestinians have used against Israelis since the founding of the state in 1948. The Palestinian authors, Walid Khalidi and Noha Ismail, explain that Palestinians are bitter because they have been denied a nation that represents their interests and values. Palestinians have had to live in squalid refugee camps, they argue, vulnerable to Israeli bombing raids, which in some cases were funded and supplied by the United States. The final viewpoint, by Thomas L. Friedman, concludes that terrorism is a natural response to the violence many Middle Easterners have witnessed and experienced since their childhoods. Leaders on both sides, Mr. Friedman believes, will have to take unprecedented steps to stop the hatred and frustration in the Middle East.

*"The Jews have come home to their Zion and have welded their city together with a fierce tightness that none...can sunder."*

# Palestine Is the Jewish Birthright

Meir Kahane

Meir Kahane is a controversial rabbi who grew up in the United States and founded the New York-based Jewish Defense League, an ultra-Zionist organization. He emigrated to Israel in 1973. Since emigration, Rabbi Kahane has become a prominent Israeli figure: he founded a political party, the Kach party, and was elected to Israel's parliament in July 1984. His party advocates expelling all Arabs from the formerly Arab territory occupied by Israel since the Six-Day War in 1967. In the following viewpoint, Rabbi Kahane explains his belief that Palestine (the land of Zion) is the Jewish birthright. Zionism led to the creation of the state of Israel which has eliminated the persecution and homelessness Jews faced before it existed. He concludes that Jews will never leave their homeland.

As you read, consider the following questions:

1. Why is Rabbi Kahane sharply critical of the United Nations?
2. Why should Jews never concede to the Arabs, according to the author?
3. Why are Israel's fighter planes and army important to Rabbi Kahane?

Meir Kahane, *Listen World, Listen Jew*. New York: The Institute of the Jewish Idea, 1978. Reprinted with the author's permission.

I am home in Jerusalem and inside sleep my children who have returned with me. Tomorrow they will go to school, climbing the hills that forever bear the footprints of those who preceded them here so many years ago—their ancestors. They will walk the hills of Jerusalem, tread its streets, mingle with their brothers and sisters from Riga and Casablanca, pray at the Wall and shyly—and then not so timidly—touch its craggy surface, add their lip prints to those who preceded them for twenty centuries and then joke in Hebrew with the bus drivers, drink their Jewish grapefruit juice as they read their Jewish newspaper and exult in their Jewish city.

"Our feet are standing within thy gates O Jerusalem," and they will never leave. This is Zionism, and the United Gentiles call it "Racist" and debate how to take my city away from me. Foolish world; sooner will the sun fail to rise tomorrow. The Jews have come home to their Zion and have welded their city together with a fierce tightness that none—least of all the humor that is the United Nations—can sunder. A people which patiently bides its time for millenia will not easily—ever—give up its state and capital....

## "Moderate" Arabs

"Time is always on the side of the tenacious; conversely it is the enemy of the weary. The constant and never ending struggle tends to erode the determination to achieve total victory and pushes tired men into the search for solutions and compromises that are often more the product of the desire to rest than that of common sense."...

The words I wrote, years ago....

And this is what is happening today with some Jews who grow weary of the eternal confrontation with the world, who fear that Zion and Zionism will go under, beneath the weight of a hostile world, and who fearfully urge "compromises" and "concessions" and "moderation"—all the things that the Arabs will construe not as goodness, but as weakness. All the things that will bring disaster down upon our heads.

"There are now 'moderate' Arabs"; "We must deal with the 'Palestinians'; "The Arabs now recognize Israel." Foolish people; forgetful people.

Forgotten are the 1967 pronouncements from Cairo, Damascus, Amman, Beirut, Baghdad, and Fatah. Forgotten are the pledges to throw us into the sea, wash Tel Aviv clean with Jewish blood and eliminate the gangster state of Israel....

Forgotten is the fact that the Haters of Zion intend nothing less than the destruction of a Jewish state of any size, shape or form. Forgotten is so much, but we remember....

Israel is not a state; it is a Decree. Israel is not a land; it is a concept. We have returned not because of Socialism or pioneers or the army—though all these will gain their place in the history of the people for their self-sacrifice and readiness to do what others were not prepared to do. We have returned because the Almighty peered at the clock of history that was being wound by the suffering of His children and decided: It is time....

Happiness for the Jew is watching the Phantoms zoom past the roofs of Zion and Jewish children shouting and waving at them. It is seeing "Jewish planes" after existing in a world for so many years in which every plane was "theirs." In a world in which planes spit their deadly bullets into Jews, their swastika markings etched into Jewish souls as they pronounced "Auschwitz" upon us....

---

## "Proud, Tough Jews"

"I want to see proud, tough Jews," [Irv Rubin, leader of the Jewish Defense League] said. "I hope to see the day when they will go into every corner, nook and cranny of this country and teach the Jew-hater a lesson he will never forget."...

Mr. Rubin met Rabbi Kahane in 1971 and remembers him saying in a speech: "'Don't sit down and have a cup of coffee with a Nazi. Don't try to be a nice guy. Smash him.'"

"It rang a bell in me," Mr. Rubin recalled.

Marcia Chambers, *The New York Times*, November 11, 1985.

---

Happiness, watching the tanks roll by, huge, awesome and, once, Russian—today, huge, awesome, and Jewish. Happiness, to see the artillery roll past—samples of the huge guns that point to Cairo and Damascus—with the knowledge that, but for them, other guns would be poised a few kilometers from our cities.

### The Jewish Army

But, above all, happiness is to watch the soldiers, our soldiers. How young they look and how tough they are. Their backs straight and their heads high and their Uzis held just so. Their faces and bodies strong and tanned and one can understand the frustration of Sadat—such Jews are, indeed, a disturbing lot.

Happiness is watching the Jewish army and knowing that the spirit of Zion cannot live without a body and that this army is the guarantor of that body's existence. And happiness is thinking, for just a moment, about what Jews have accomplished in the few years since they returned home. From thousands to millions of Jews; from ghettos to cities and farms that are all Jewish; from a motley medley of foreign tongues to the resurrection of Hebrew—and how sweet it is to hear the military commands and the most technical of phrases spoken in the tongue of Abraham and the Book of Genesis....

Happiness is knowing that a huge mistake has been made—that Israel is not thirty years old but three thousand and thirty years old, and that this State is only a continuum of the last one with a mere matter of two thousand years in between due to unavoidable Exile.

Happiness is watching the non-Jews looking at a Jewish parade in the Jewish capital city of the Jewish State. Happiness is knowing that most of the non-Jewish countries who have consulates and embassies in the City of David boycott the Independence Day parade lest their presence be construed as recognition of the Jewishness of the City—and not giving one solitary hoot whether they show up or not!

## No Longer a Minority

Happiness is watching young Jewish children who never knew what it meant to be a minority and never heard the words "zhid" or "kike" or "yahud." Happiness is knowing that if anyone did call them that, he would find his face attached to the end of a Jewish fist. Happiness is watching the soldiers with beards and yarmulkas showing that mastering the intricacies of a mere sub-machine gun is child's play for a Talmudic scholar.

Happiness is watching the parade begin in East Jerusalem where for 19 years no Jew was allowed to go. Happiness is standing on the roof of your apartment and watching the formations of planes come from far off in the distance and seeing the hills of Benjamin and Ephraim, slowly beginning to sprout housing and Jewish settlements; knowing that, when next you stand on that roof, the hills would be filled with countless more Jews.

He who does not believe that the rise of the State of Israel is the hand of G-d is not only a non-believer; he is also blind. If this rebirth of a nation and state and language from the clutching jaws of the seventy wolves is not a miracle, then there are indeed no miracles. If the renaissance of a people in the face of every logic and sanity is not Divine decree then the Spring that brings rejuvenation to the dead earth is not Divine and the life that emerges from the mother's womb is profane and natural.

Happiness is walking in Zion and embracing your father Abraham. Happiness, for the Jew, is Zionism. Are you listening world?

"The ancient Jewish possession of Palestine did not...give contemporary Jews an overarching political right which negated the political rights of the Palestinians."

# Palestine Is Not the Jewish Birthright

Walid Khalidi

Zionism, the belief in a Jewish right to a homeland, is an injustice to Palestinians who were displaced when the Jews chose Palestine as their homeland, according to Walid Khalidi. In the following viewpoint, Mr. Khalidi uses the hypothetical situation of two nations with conflicting national aspirations to illustrate that the Palestinians' negative reaction to Zionism was a natural one. Palestinians have a right to their own state, he believes, and Israel's annexation of East Jerusalem, an area where Arabs are in the majority, ruins chances for peace. Mr. Khalidi is the founder of the Institute for Palestine Studies and is currently a research fellow at Harvard University's Center for Middle Eastern Studies.

As you read, consider the following questions:

1. Why did the Palestinians oppose Zionism from the start, according to the author?
2. What painful experiences have shaped what Mr. Khalidi terms the "new generation" of Palestinian activism?
3. What does the author mean by the "Palestinian Diaspora"?

Walid Khalidi, "A Palestinian Perspective on the Arab-Israeli Conflict," *Journal of Palestine Studies*, Summer 1985. Reprinted with permission of the *Journal of Palestine Studies*, Washington, DC.

Palestinian and Arab reactions to Zionism and Israel are often presented as so bizarre as to lie beyond the domain of human reason. Atavistic hypotheses are adduced to explain these reactions, and the Palestinians are transposed into the successors of the historic European tormentors of the Jewish people. Such perceptions are possible only if one lapses into historical amnesia.

To be sure, incursions into the historical record have been preludes to the delegitimization of the other. But this need not be the case. One could look backward in order to look forward. Humankind is driven by circumstances beyond its control. But it also impinges on its environment with more or less willfulness, for which, to that extent, it is accountable.

## Zionism's Choices

Zionism was born in Eastern Europe in the last decades of the nineteenth century in response to the twin challenges of persecution and assimilation—but phenomena beyond the control of any single people. Diagnosis by Zionist ideologues, however, led to the prescription of Jewish statehood as the guarantor of Jewish cultural survival and national fulfillment....

Had the Zionists chosen an *uninhabited* territorial locus, all presumably would have gone well. Had they chosen inhabited territory X other than Palestine, the Middle East would presumably be a happier place today. But as likely as not, you would still have had to listen to the sermon of an unacknowledged spokesman of territory X....

One could, if one were so inclined, absolve Zionism of responsibilities under the "morality of intent." One would have to be very Christian indeed to absolve it of responsibilities under the "morality of effect."

Now, at the time of the advent of Zionism, the Palestinians constituted the cumulative human residue, ethnic layer upon ethnic layer, of the admixture of all the peoples, (including the ancient Hebrews and their descendants), who had entered and left Palestine since time immemorial.

## Palestinian Birthright

In Palestinian eyes, the Palestinian birthright to their country was as pristine as anyone else's to theirs. And, as you might surmise, the Palestinians had a somewhat different perspective on the subject than the Zionists themselves.

No, the Palestinians could not endorse the Zionist argument from Divine Law. They were unaware that Allah meant them, or any people, to concede their country to others.

No, the Palestinians could not endorse the Zionist argument from Natural Law based on past Jewish suffering, if that meant conceding that the Jews had a greater need for Palestine than the Palestinians themselves....

118

No, the ancient Jewish possession of Palestine did not, after a lapse of 2,000 years, give contemporary Jews an overarching political right which negated the political rights of the Palestinians themselves.

These arguments of Zionism have never lacked plausibility for Western third parties. But Zionist plausibility was, and is, in the ear and in the guilt of the Western listener. And, as the Arab saying goes, to count the lashes is not to receive them.

From the start, the Palestinians recognized in Zionism their dispossessor and heard in all the Zionist arguments only a brief for their own delegitimization. So the Palestinians countered delegitimization with delegitimization....

The exponents of new Palestinian activism were a new generation haunted by 1948, seared to the soul by the humiliation of exile, of camp life, and the indifference of the world. Their aim was not to establish a Palestinian state in the West Bank and East Jerusalem and the Gaza Strip—then still in Arab hands—but to redress the intolerable, unforgettable injustice of 1948....

## Importance of Sovereignty

The *raison d'être* [reason for existence] of Zionism was to establish one place under the sun where the Jews were in the majority; and the key to Jewish national fulfillment was seen to be Jewish sovereignty. Both conditions are amply fulfilled within the 1967 borders of Israel.

---

### Zionist Hijacking

The whole country of Palestine has been hijacked by the Zionists. The Zionist Jews of Europe, America and elsewhere are in, two million Palestinians are out. Palestinian hijackings will stop only when the Palestinians' human right to return to their land is recognized.

M.T. Mehdi, Letter to *The New York Times*, October 17, 1985.

---

All God's human creatures need a mailbox, a turf they can call their own. All God's animal creatures need their den-areas, be they branches of a tree or a heap of rocks.

The key to Palestinian fulfillment is not the management of the sewers of Hebron and Nablus, just as the key to Jewish fulfillment was not the management of the sewers of Tel Aviv. The key to Palestinian national fulfillment is sovereignty.

The total number of Palestinians is equivalent to the total populations of some twenty member states in the UN. Literacy among Palestinians is higher than it is in eighty percent of the members of the UN.

Just as all Jews in their Diaspora [exile from Palestine] would not or could not live in Israel, not all Palestinians in their Diaspora could or would live in the Palestinian state. But just as Israel works its magic on the Jews of the Diaspora, the sovereign state of Palestine (within the 1967 frontiers) will work its magic on the Palestinian Diaspora.

Let us have on the West Bank, in East Jerusalem, and in the Gaza Strip, and indeed in the Golan and in the whole of Lebanon (in the immortal words of Caspar Weinberger), "a form of government that enables the people to choose the kind of government they wish."...

## Jerusalem's Common Heritage

A word about Jerusalem. Jerusalem is not and cannot be the eternal capital of this or that people. Jerusalem is the eternal capital of Humankind.

Judaism has no monopoly on the Hebrew prophets. They too are the common heritage of Humankind. Ironically, Islam, alone of the three monotheistic faiths, embraces the other two in its ken.

Jerusalem was not torn in two by a concrete wall erected before 1967. Jerusalem has not been united by the pulling down of that wall. The concrete wall was but a ramshackle barrier symbolizing an inner, more formidable wall.

Let us stop paying homage to an alibi. Let us stop the pretense that the forcible annexation and absorption by Israel of East Jerusalem is a healing process....

Access to the Jewish holy places had never been an issue in itself before it fell victim to the political struggle engulfing the whole land. Within the concept of a twin ecumenical capital, much can be done to dam the tears and staunch the wounds of all....

### Negotiating Ploys

It is no service to this or that Arab capital to bully it to break Arab ranks. It is even less sensible to entice this or that Palestinian Uncle Tom to deliver a constituency he does not possess. The Palestinian constituency is made up of two halves: the Palestinians of the occupied territories and the Palestinians of the Diaspora.

In spite of the current PLO disarray there is no substitute for talks between the PLO and Israel. There is nothing sacred in [former US Secretary of State Henry] Kissinger's straightjacket proviso for unilateral, prior and unreciprocated recognition by the PLO of Israel. Let us recognize this proviso for what it is: a ploy to keep the PLO away from the conference table. It is only the adversaries who can or should give reciprocal recognition to each other. But no Palestinian leadership inside or outside the PLO can break Arab ranks.

There is no substitute for a general, political, regional, integrated, conceptual framework, and a multi-track, multi-issue approach. By a multi-track, multi-issue approach is meant quiet, patient, intelligent, inventive, politically purposeful dialogue with all the key protagonists: local, regional and global; simultaneously addressing at different levels of publicity and salience the issues of Palestinian self-determination, Lebanon and the Golan. If the horrendous mess in Lebanon points to anything, it points to the absence of such a conceptual framework and such an approach....

## Palestinian Nationalism

The one dimension that the Israelis refuse to see in the West Bank situation is the force of Palestinian nationalism, despite the blatant evidence that it exists and is growing and, unsurprisingly, that the more the Israelis deny it the more they are encouraging it. In other words, the Israelis insist on viewing the West Bank problem as a "technical" one of people and territory and their administration: they refuse to acknowledge that the ideological interaction of people, land, culture and common historic experience—the very roots of Zionism, in fact!—is alive and well among the Palestinian people.

David Seymour, *New Outlook: Middle East Monthly*, December 1984/January 1985.

It deeply grieves me and disturbs me to say that the Arab debate about the United States no longer concerns whether the United States is evenhanded or not, whether it is a mediator, an honest broker, or a referee. The debate in the Arab world concerns whether the United States is structurally capable of being evenhanded in the Palestinian problem and the Arab-Israeli conflict. No one is asking the United States to choose between Israel and the Arabs. But every Palestinian and Arab is fully entitled to ask the United States: Are you supporting the state of Israel or the empire of *Eretz* Israel?

*"The PLO...has proved incapable of disengaging itself from very militant policies accompanied by terror, based...on a strategy of terror."*

# The PLO Is a Terrorist Organization

**Shimon Peres**

Since the state of Israel was founded in 1948, it has refused to negotiate with PLO leaders until the PLO rejects terrorism. That position is expressed in the following viewpoint written by Shimon Peres, who was elected prime minister of Israel in July 1984. He argues that the Palestinians have had several opportunities for negotiating a peaceful and fair settlement of their grievances but have always ruined their chances by resorting to a militant and often violent position. Both Jews and Palestinians have national rights to the land of Palestine, he believes, but neither group can live in peace until Palestinians are willing to negotiate and compromise.

As you read, consider the following questions:

1. How has the Palestinian position caused five wars since the founding of the state of Israel in 1948, according to Mr. Peres?
2. Why does the author doubt the PLO's sincerity when their leaders call for negotiations?
3. Why does Mr. Peres believe time is running out for peace negotiations in the Middle East?

Shimon Peres, "A Season of Promise in the Middle East," excerpts from a speech given to the American Enterprise Institute, Washington, D.C., October 18, 1985. Reprinted with permission of the American Enterprise Institute from *The AEI Memorandum*, Fall 1985.

The State of Israel has existed for thirty-seven years. The Zionist movement started 100 years ago. The Jewish Awakening came simultaneously with the Arab Awakening. The two movements could have met at the same time and the same place in agreement and understanding, but alas, instead and maybe contrary to the wishes of the two sides, surely to our own wish, it became a confrontation that garnered hostility, suspicion, militancy, and a very heavy toll of lost life.

The basic conflict started between the Palestinian people and us. The Palestinian position, from our standpoint, caused five wars over the past thirty-seven years. Naturally, we are very critical of the Palestinian leadership and the Palestinian position. In retrospect, if the Palestinians had agreed to a Palestinian state in 1947 and 1948 as decided upon by the United Nations, maybe the wars, the confrontation, the hostility, and the need for a complex solution could have been prevented.

### Palestinian Leadership

Time and again, we could have solved the problems. Time and again, an opportunity was born and killed. For the Palestinian people we have nothing but the wish that they be able to live in accordance with their own traditions and hopes. But our attitude toward the Palestinian leadership, which has never recognized realities, timing, and opportunities, is understandably negative.

The experience has been very costly to Palestinian life, to Jewish life, to Arab life. It is frustrating and disappointing because most of the Arab countries who launched wars against Israel did so not because they were in conflict with Israel but because they tried to solve by force the conflict with the Palestinians.

Many people ask us, If the PLO changes its policies, will you be ready to negotiate with them? Alas, the question before us is a different one: not what *if* this happens, but *can* it really happen?

In our judgment, the PLO by its experience, by its divisions, and by its inclination has proved incapable of disengaging itself from very militant policies accompanied by terror, based in fact on a strategy of terror. Therefore, it cannot further the cause and destinies of the Palestinian people.

### Talking Peace and Killing People

I believe [Jordan's] King Hussein tried to reach an agreement with the PLO, in the hope of divorcing the PLO from its past and going together in the direction of peace. I tend to believe that this was a sincere effort of the King. But while an agreement was signed, a direction was not decided upon. Apparently the King and the PLO decided to go together but have yet to agree on which way to go. Although the King tried to lead the PLO in the direction of peace and negotiation, the PLO may have tried to lead the King in a direction of confrontation....

123

If the PLO had really decided to seek peace, why increase the terror, the killing, the tension, at such a difficult time, trying to outrage the Israeli people by talking peace in one place and killing people in another?...

[From] January 1985 [to October 1985], the PLO has initiated 117 attempts to kill people—men, women, and children—endangering the process that they have supposedly agreed upon with Jordan.

---

### Abysmally Bad

It is the Palestinians who have suffered most from the Arab politics of self-delusion, which has reached its fullest flower in the person of Yasser Arafat, chairman of the Palestine Liberation Organization. Arafat, to put the matter bluntly, has been an abysmally bad leader for his people....

Arafat has failed in the basic obligation of a political leader. He has refused to make choices—to choose honestly whether the PLO will be a military organization, trying to overcome Israel by force of arms, or a political organization trying to negotiate the best deal possible for its constituents. Instead, he has tried to have it both ways—to talk peace and war at once. The clearest sign of this is Arafat's maddening game about whether he recognizes Israel's right to exist. When meeting with Westerners, he will hint, suggest, imply (but never quite say directly) that he does; when meeting with Arabs, he will generally spout rejectionist rhetoric. It was never clear to me, in three years of covering Arafat, whom he thought he was kidding.

David Ignatius, *The Washington Monthly*, November 1984.

---

As I look back from 1947 to today, my own conclusions are that peace is needed, that it is possible to achieve, that there is a Palestinian issue, that we have to solve this issue in an honorable manner, and that the only way to solve it is by peaceful negotiations, by diplomatic means. There is no military solution to the fate of hundreds of thousands of people. A solution must be found; we need it urgently, and they need it urgently.

### Obstacles to Peace

But the greatest obstacle to peace, paradoxically, is the organization that is supposed to represent the Palestinians. I ask myself seriously, Do the Palestinians on the West Bank support the PLO? I would say yes. They support the ideas of the PLO, but with a qualification, a provision. They are ready to support the ideas of the PLO if the PLO will lead to a solution. But if the PLO will only repeat the agonies and tragedies that they have experienced in the past, they will not follow the PLO.

I believe we have to start to negotiate. Israel is ready to negotiate directly with a Jordanian delegation or, alternatively, with a Jordanian-Palestinian delegation, or a Jordanian delegation that comprises Palestinian members....

The issue is this: Can we get out of our way terror, extremism, and self-delusions? Peace will never come to the Middle East unless the parties recognize that peace has a cost very much like war. In war, in order to win, you have to be ready to sacrifice the lives of many people. To accomplish peace, you must be ready to make compromises. Don't go to a negotiating table unless you are ready to do so.

We feel very strongly that time is running out, because in the Middle East time is arms. More and more countries are buying more and more arms, arms that are more and more lethal, clouding the very narrow skies of peace in the region.

We must move ahead promptly, without hesitation, with a readiness to listen, each to the other party, and finally to compromise on a middle way. And yet, contrary to our inclinations, we should not embark on too many discussions about the nature of the solution.

Believe me, the archives of the Middle East are full of very elaborate and imaginative plans, but until now they have produced archives and not realities. What we need is not additional plans. What we really need right now is an opening, a beginning. The real problem today is not the last step on the road to peace but the first move in that direction.

### Third Solution

I cannot think of any plan that will satisfy and not antagonize the two parties, one that will allow them to come to terms. We have to be ambiguous, all of us, about the solution and definite about the beginning. Let us meet; let us discuss, remembering that the final plan of successful negotiations will never resemble the plan of one side or another side but will always be a third solution, not thought of before the negotiations started.

I believe if terrorism, militancy, and obstructionism are removed from the road of peace, we may be facing today, for the first time, a real opportunity to accommodate and settle the most pressing and important issue between us and the Arab people. I feel very strongly that in spite of the evident difficulties, we may be facing a season for peace. As far as Israel is concerned, we would not like to miss this season of promise.

*"The only hope for real peace...is for the Israelis to initiate serious discussions with the Palestine Liberation Organization [PLO]."*

# Israel Must Recognize the PLO

Noha Ismail

Negotiations for peace in the Middle East have been complicated by the refusal of Israel and the United States to negotiate with the Palestine Liberation Organization (PLO), according to Noha Ismail. Ms. Ismail was born in Palestine. Her family lost their home and moved to Egypt when the state of Israel was created. She came to the United States in 1970 and is the state coordinator of the American-Arab Anti-Discrimination Commmittee in Minnesota. In the following viewpoint, she argues that the plight of the homeless Palestinians has been ignored by other nations. Only a sovereign Palestinian state can protect Palestinians and restore their national honor, she concludes.

As you read, consider the following questions:

1. How has the origin of the Arab-Israeli conflict been distorted, according to the author?
2. What does the author say has happened to Palestinians since the state of Israel was created?
3. What does the author believe is the only hope for peace in the Middle East?

Noha Ismail, "Until Palestinians Have Homeland, Mideast Peace Won't Come," *St. Paul Pioneer Press and Dispatch*, June 2, 1985. Reprinted with the author's permission.

If events in the Middle East seem rather complicated, it is only because the crux of the problem—the origin of the Arab-Israeli conflict—has been distorted and twisted beyond recognition. One cannot possibly understand what is happening today without first confronting the historic events that transformed Arab Palestine into Jewish Israel in 1948.

After World War II the western world, which had long tormented and abused the Jewish people, was anxious to make amends. The Zionist movement was calling for the establishment of a national homeland in Palestine for the Jews of the world. The horrors of Hitler's Germany dramatized their need for a refuge where they could take control of their lives. Eager to end the suffering of the victims of the Holocaust, the Zionist leaders and the western world chose to overlook the fact that Palestine was already a homeland for another group of people who had been living there for centuries.

## Dehumanized Palestinians

So that an "exclusively" Jewish state could be created, it became necessary to shove the Palestinians across the border like a herd of sheep, to make room for a whole new society of transplanted Jews. To camouflage the moral issue and establish an aura of justification around this action, a systematic campaign to dehumanize the Palestinians was launched.

We Palestinians suddenly became the primitive nomads roaming the desert; we were the illiterate, hungry mass of refugees; we were the hateful embittered Arabs; and, finally, we became the abominable, wild-eyed terrorists.

Those who idealize the "miracle in the desert," admire Israel's accomplishments and romanticize its kibbutzim may find it difficult to admit that beneath the glamour lies a tragedy of another people who suffered for no reason, and who were made to pay the price of a crime that others have committed.

## Stateless and Forgotten

Today, in the golden age of people's rights and self-determination, the Palestinian is determined but not self-determining. One-third of us are living in bondage under the Israeli occupation, robbed of our sense of purpose and worth as human beings. Another third are living in fear in squalid, infamous camps in Syria and Lebanon —terrified of venturing outside the camps lest we be rounded-up, imprisoned, kidnapped or massacred. The rest are, like myself, living in exile and scattered all over the world.

This fragmentation has ravished our lives. Being a Palestinian means that you are an outsider no matter where you live. It means that you are an alien, a refugee and a burden. It means that you are doomed to being stateless, faceless, excluded and forgotten.

I belong to a people with a distinctly Palestinian consciousness. We share a common heritage, history and culture. Yet none of us can return to the country that binds us together. We hurt, and the intensity of our anguish cannot be negated by those who deny our existence or dismiss us as pariah refugees or bloodthirsty terrorists.

We are human beings who happen to be Palestinian. We are doctors, scholars, teachers, housewives, students, poets and clerical workers. We are mothers and lost forgotten children. We feel pain

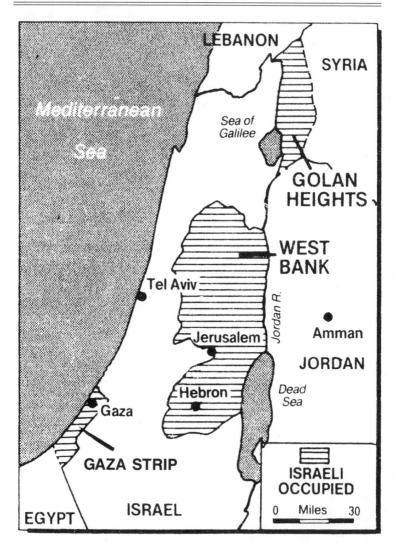

**Territory occupied by Israel since 1967.**

Horn in The Christian Science Monitor © 1985 TCSPS

when we suffer, laugh when we feel happy, and dream when we contemplate the future. We are ordinary folk who yearn for a homeland and a place under the sun that we can call our own. Surely the Israelis can understand the importance of this process, because it is one that they themselves have endured.

Like the Jews in their diaspora, we have been forced to conclude that only a sovereign independent state can assure us control over our destinies. Most of us realize that we cannot restore Arab Palestine. What we seek is a part in which many of us still live on the West Bank and Gaza. A separate state would end the anomalies of displacement and exile. It cannot represent full justice, nor would it undo the harm done over so many years. But it would fulfill our dreams and restore to us our nationhood and human dignity.

Addressing legitimate Palestinian grievances through a fair solution to our historical and existential problems is vital in getting us to come to terms with the Israelis. The only hope for real peace and security is for the Israelis to initiate serious discussions with the Palestine Liberation Organization. Arab states have no right to speak on our behalf.

## No Substitute for PLO

The Zionist enemy has succeeded in using the weapon of land sequestration, but has not until now—despite its terrorist policies, its many massacres and its acts of brutality—succeeded in uprooting that part of our people from its national soil. It may be said that the fact that our people have remained on our national soil constitutes the most effective weapon we possess to combat the policy of creeping dispossession of the land. Furthermore, our masses in the occupied homeland have played a prominent role in frustrating attempts to create a substitute for the PLO. It has become impossible for the enemy to find anyone with any mass following willing to negotiate with them or speak in place of the PLO.

George Habash, *Journal of Palestine Studies,* Summer 1985.

Palestinian leaders are receptive to the idea of an international peace conference to which *all* interested parties would be invited. PLO leader Yasser Arafat has openly indicated his willingness to recognize Israel within the framework of bilateral recognition between two sovereign states. His remarks have been almost ignored in the mainstream American press. The U.S. government cannot ask the Palestinians to recognize Israel without a quid pro quo, such as Israeli recognition of Palestinian national rights.

It is important to realize that a Palestinian gain does not mean an Israeli loss. Depending on how it evolves, a Palestinian state could be in the best interest of both Israel and the United States. Peace is possible only on the basis of mutual respect and dignity.

*"It will take some Israeli to bring out the moderate in Yasir Arafat. And it will take an overture by Arafat to bring out the moderate in many Israelis."*

# Israel and the Palestinians Must Compromise

Thomas L. Friedman

The author of the following viewpoint, Thomas L. Friedman, was chief of *The New York Times* bureau in Beirut, Lebanon from 1982 to 1984 and is currently the bureau chief in Jerusalem. Extremist nationalists have the upper hand in the Middle East now, Mr. Friedman argues, because they have simplified and distorted the issues in a way that appeals to deep and ancient nationalist passions. Such simplified views make it possible for Jews and Arabs to condone terrorist raids which kill innocent people. He concludes the viewpoint by contrasting his two impressions of what the future of the Middle East may be. One possibility is that both sides become more moderate and find a fair solution to their conflicting national interests. The darker possibility is that they remain intransigent and future generations grow up violent and embittered by the hatred they have witnessed.

As you read, consider the following questions:

1. Why does Mr. Friedman think it is important that most Jews now call the West Bank area Judea and Samaria?
2. What agenda should the Palestinian Arabs adopt, according to the author?

Although political moderates probably remain a majority in the Middle East, they are finding it increasingly difficult to defend their values. My overwhelming impression is that, throughout the area, the moderates are on the run.

I saw moderation on the run in the recent Israeli election campaign, when Rabbi Meir Kahane, an anti-Arab racist, was able to win a seat in the Israeli Knesset, while his ideological opposite, Lova Eliav, who campaigned on a one-man ticket calling for peaceful coexistence with the Arabs, fell far short of the minimum number of votes needed to secure a parliamentary seat.

I saw tolerance smothered on a Friday afternoon in June 1982, when I came home to my Beirut apartment house to find that it had been demolished. Two groups of Palestinian refugees had gotten into a fight over who would take over the eight-story building, and the group that lost simply blew up the whole place, killing my Palestinian driver's wife and two daughters, who happened to be inside my apartment at the time. I will always remember my driver, Muhammed, sitting in the back of a firetruck, weeping and repeating to himself: "It isn't fair, I am a man of peace, I never carried a gun in my life."...

These are but a few examples. I could go on. The question is: Why is this happening? Why is it that those who hold the most extreme, the most hard-line, the most uncompromising positions in the Middle East seem so strong of late? What is the source of their strength, and why do they seem to be setting the agenda for us all?...

## The Importance of Language

Extremists, and all those in the Middle East who reject compromise solutions, are gaining strength today because they understand much better than the moderates the importance of language and agendas. They recognize much more clearly than their opponents that determining how people describe their world, how they see their alternatives, is where the real power lies.

For instance, after the Six-Day War of 1967, elements from the extreme nationalist Israeli movement Gush Emunim were able to generate enough pressure on a succession of hesitant and divided Israeli Cabinets to get the biblical names of Judea and Samaria imposed officially on the territory known in modern times as the West Bank. The new names, repeated in all Israeli radio and television broadcasts and in all Government documents, naturally carried over into the daily language of politics—to such an extent that, during the recent election campaign, even the Labor Party leader, Shimon Peres, referred to the territory as Judea and Samaria.

The Gush Emunim people know that to name something is to own it. They know that any Israeli who calls the area Judea and Samaria can never really deny the argument that this territory is the biblical cradle of Judaism; that, hence, it is Jewish land, and that

131

to return it to Arab sovereignty would involve a kind of sacrilege. To call it the West Bank has much more neutral overtones and leaves open the possibility of compromise....

## New Agenda

Imagine how different the debate might be if the agenda were shaped differently—if, for instance, the debate were over the ultimate character of Israel. The choice then would be between whether Israel should absorb one million hostile Palestinian Arabs and eventually lose its Jewish character, or whether Israel should find a safe way to divest itself of the West Bank and retain its Jewish character. As a Peace Now activist said to me, that would be a much better field for debate, but it is not the field the Israeli moderates are fighting on, which is one reason they are on the run.

---

### Mutual Recognition

Both the Palestinian and the Jewish peoples possess legitimate claims to the land they inhabit. Certainly neither is about to give it up.

Under the circumstances, for anyone who cares about a solution to the problem, throwing around names like "racist" or "terrorist" must be seen as counterproductive....

What is needed is clear: mutual recognition leading to direct talks involving Israel and the PLO.

Dennis Fischman, *The Guardian*, January 8, 1986.

---

The same situation holds true in the Arab world. The Arab extremists have imposed an agenda defining as treasonous any Arab accommodation with Israel that contradicts the objective of establishing a Palestinian state in "all" of Palestine. But imagine how different the position of Palestinian moderates would be if they had been able to convince Palestinians that the question on the agenda was not how to get back "everything" but "how to relieve the homelessness of our people and satisfy our minimal demands for national self-determination." Approaching the future with that agenda might have led the Palestinian leaders to make some very different choices at critical stages in their recent history.

### Private Intentions

It could be said, "Who cares what Shimon Peres calls the West Bank? The fact is, he is privately for compromise, and will prove it if given the chance." Or, "Who cares what the P.L.O. board of directors forces Arafat to say in public? When push comes to shove, it is his private intentions that will matter."

It doesn't always work that way. I learned that covering the April

1983 talks in Amman between Arafat and King Hussein on the subject of the Reagan Plan for some form of federation between the West Bank and Jordan. There was no question that Arafat wanted to go along with the Jordanian monarch and agree to negotiations on the American President's proposal. But when Arafat flew to Kuwait to convince the P.L.O. central committee members of the wisdom of going along with some form of the Reagan initiative, they overwhelmingly rejected his arguments.

The fault lay squarely with Arafat. After all those years of talking out of both sides of his mouth, after all those years of using the language of extremism in public and the language of moderation in private, Arafat had abandoned the public debate to his hard-line rivals. When the time came for him to marshal a constituency for compromise within his own movement, the support was not there. He had never shaped it....

## Importance of Simplicity

Political extremists and religious fanatics understand the importance not only of language and agenda but of simplicity....They are willing and able to simplify their positions into short clichés that divert attention from the complexities and constraints of the real world. Extremists have always been much better at exploiting the media, understanding as they do that the media responds to simplicity, to black and white....

When people do not make distinctions, killing and extremist violence become so much easier to carry out and to rationalize. In fact, these kinds of oversimplifications pave the way for extremist violence. They are what enables a Palestinian to leave a bomb on a "Zionist" bus that will kill "Zionist" soldiers and "Zionist" civilians, "Zionist" peace activists and "Zionist" warmongers alike. ("Who cares? They're just Zionists.")

Such statements were what enabled the Druse to lob shells into Christian East Beirut day after day, never caring whether they hit militiamen or civilians. They were all Christians, and that was enough. Such statements laid the groundwork for the massacre at the Palestinian refugee camps of Sabra and Shatila. The Christian Phalangist militia, and, to a certain extent, some Israelis, had so dehumanized the Palestinians, labeling everything they touched as "terrorist"—terrorist tanks, but also terrorist hospitals, terrorist doctors and terrorist nurses—that they could no longer distinguish between true terrorists, guerrilla fighters and innocent women and children. They did not even realize that the part of Shatila where the massacre began was populated by many poor Lebanese Shiites, who had been attracted by cheap housing in the camp....

Extremists are not an aberration confined to the society's fringe. People who resort to extremist violence are often acting on feelings widely shared by their compatriots. Sometimes the only difference

THIS IS A RAID →

THIS IS A RETALIATORY RAID ←

THIS IS A REACTION TO THE RETALIATORY RAID →

THIS IS A RETALIATION FOR THE REACTION TO THE RETALIATORY RAID ←

THIS IS A RAID AVENGING THE RETALIATION FOR THE REACTION TO THE RETALIATORY RAID ↗

...WELCOME TO THE HOLY LAND

Reprinted by Permission of United Features Syndicate, Inc.

between the extremist and the average citizen is that the extremist takes the frustrations and anger of the people around him and plays them out to their limits and beyond....

Anyone who says the Jewish terrorists in Israel are a fringe element is fooling himself, and there are polls that make this clear. One poll, taken by the newspaper Ha'aretz after the 27 men were arrested, found that 31.8 percent of the Israeli public regarded the terrorists' actions as either fully or partly justified. It was revealed in the court papers that, in some instances, when the terrorist ringleaders visited a Jewish house to recruit a new member and the person they came to see was out, they would make their appeal to whoever was home. The image of secret underground meetings in caves by candlelight does not apply.

### Israeli Sentiment

An Israeli friend of mine told me of a discussion he had with his maid about the Jewish terrorists; he asked her what she thought of them. The woman, whose family had emigrated from the Jewish community of Morocco, said it was terrible that they had been arrested. After all, she said, it wasn't fair that the Arabs should be able to have an underground and the Jews not. The sentiment may be simple, but it has an intuitive appeal to a substantial portion of the Israeli public.

Perhaps, then, what is most worrisome about such developments in the Middle East is not the rise of the extremist fringe but the rise of an extremist center. As extremist violence engulfs more and more people's lives, it gains more and more recruits. Behind every extremist act, one can usually find an amorphous body of feelings and attitudes that supports it to a significant degree....

By refusing to recognize Israel and negotiate with it directly, the Arabs have only strengthened Israeli fanatics like Rabbi Kahane, enabling them to play on the legitimate fears and security concerns of the Israeli public. The Arabs have always deluded themselves into believing that they would get what they wanted out of Israel by organizing pressure against it from the outside. But the road to a Palestinian homeland does not run through United Nations resolutions, or hijackings, or even warfare. It runs through the Israeli public and Israeli democracy. There is still a majority for compromise in Israel, but it has to be activated through dialogue and recognition. It is only the Arabs, I believe, who can bring Kahane down—by negotiating with Israel on a political settlement.

## Garden of Fanaticism

As for the link between extremism and insensitivity, look at the garden of fanaticism the Israelis have been cultivating in southern Lebanon, whose population is roughly 80 percent Shiite Moslem and 20 percent Christian. From almost the day the Israeli Army invaded the area, its policy has been a chronicle of insensitivity and error. This has created an extremist Shiite opposition among people who only two years earlier greeted the Israelis with rice and flowers as their liberators from the capricious rule of the P.L.O. Instead of seeking to work quietly through the legitimate Shiite leadership in the south, represented by the Amal militia, the Israelis imposed Maj. Saad Haddad, a Greek Orthodox Christian, as their effective governor general of the whole region—a serious affront to the Shiites, who probably could have served just as effectively as an anti-P.L.O. force....

The end result of all of this is that the Shiites of southern Lebanon have become the sworn enemies of Israel as much as of the P.L.O....

## Hope for a Solution

Given the increasing velocity of extremist violence in the Middle East, one might well ask whether there is any hope for moderate solutions to the problems of the region. When I need a dose of optimism, I think about Moshe Dayan and Sharm el-Sheikh.

For years, the Israeli general and war hero would declare, "Better Israel should not have peace with Egypt and keep Sharm el-Sheikh than give up Sharm el-Sheikh and have peace with Egypt." Sharm el-Sheikh, it may be recalled, was the little base at the southern tip of the Sinai Peninsula that General Dayan thought was more important to Israel's survival than peace with its strongest Arab enemy.

Then Sadat came to Israel. He extended his hand in friendship, and Moshe Dayan discovered things in himself and in his former enemy that he never knew were there. Suddenly, the world looked different to him. Suddenly, he had a completely different agenda.

Suddenly, Sharm el-Sheikh looked very small.

There is a very important lesson here. We have an enormous power to shape each other, and when you create a new dynamic between people, all kinds of new things become possible.

People I meet often say to me, "You've talked to Yasir Arafat. Tell me, is he really a moderate?" I always have the same answer: "I don't know, and, more important, Yasir Arafat doesn't know. And he will not know until he is tested." It took Anwar Sadat to bring out the moderate in Moshe Dayan and Menachem Begin, and it will take some Israeli to bring out the moderate in Yasir Arafat. And it will take an overture by Arafat to bring out the moderate in many Israelis. But, as Sadat showed, people can change; stereotypes can crumble....

### Horrific Scene

Of the many horrific scenes I took away from Beirut, there is one in particular that I will never forget. It took place in Shatila a few days after the massacre. The Red Cross workers had come into the camp, had collected the bodies and were burying them in a mass grave in an empty field. They had dug a long, 12-foot-deep trench and were carrying the bodies down there, one by one. They would lay out a row of bodies, pour white lime over them to deaden the stench, and cover them with dirt. Then they would put another layer on top of these, and so on, until the grave was filled.

As I stood watching, I noticed, next to me, a little Palestinian boy. He was wearing a red shirt and shorts, and was sitting on a small stool. He could not have been more than 8 or 9 years old, and I remember he had a white gauze mask to fend off the stench, but it was too large for him and had fallen down around his neck. His eyes were full of tears. He was obviously watching members of his own family being buried, maybe his entire family for all I know.

I remember looking at that little boy and thinking that no one, let alone a child, should ever have to watch such a wretched scene as this burial. I remember wondering what lifelong scars were being formed right then and there on that boy's mind, what desire for revenge was being planted in his heart.

### Cycle of Revenge

This is how it happens, I thought to myself. This is how the cycle keeps going. One generation watches another go to its miserable, miserable grave, and a new generation of avengers, of extremists, of people unable to make distinctions, is born.

What I hope is that the lesson of Anwar Sadat's initiative and Moshe Dayan's response will be learned before too long, and save that little boy from his destiny as another hate-filled extremist. What I fear is that his scars and his passions will win the day and set the agenda for us all.

# Recognizing Ethnocentrism

Ethnocentrism is the attitude or tendency of people to view their own race, religion, culture, group, or nation as superior to others, and to judge others on that basis. An American, whose custom is to eat with a fork or spoon, would be making an ethnocentric statement when saying, "The Chinese custom of eating with chopsticks is stupid."

Ethnocentrism has promoted much misunderstanding and conflict. It emphasizes cultural and religious differences and the notion that one's national institutions or group customs are superior.

Ethnocentrism limits people's ability to be objective and to learn from others. Education in the truest sense stresses the similarities of the human condition throughout the world and the basic equality and dignity of all people.

Most of the following statements are taken from the viewpoints in this book. Some have other origins. Consider each statement carefully. *Mark E for any statement you think is ethnocentric. Mark N for any statement you think is not ethnocentric. Mark U if you are undecided about any statement.*

If you are doing this activity as a member of a class or group, compare your answers with those of other class or group members. Be able to defend your answers. You may discover that others will come to different conclusions than you. Listening to the reasons others present for their answers may give you valuable insights in recognizing ethnocentric statements.

If you are reading this book alone, ask others if they agree with your answers. You too will find this interaction very valuable.

*E = ethnocentric*
*N = not ethnocentric*
*U = undecided*

1. My children will drink their Jewish grapefruit juice as they read their Jewish newspaper and exult in their Jewish city.

2. The Jews have come home to their Zion and have welded their city together with a fierce tightness that none can sunder.

3. Zionism was born in Eastern Europe in the last decades of the nineteenth century in response to the twin challenges of persecution and assimiliation.

4. Israel is not a state; it is a Decree. Israel is not a land; it is a concept.

5. The total number of Palestinians is equivalent to the total populations of some twenty member states in the UN.

6. We have returned because the Almighty peered at the clock of history that was being wound by the suffering of His children and decided: It is time.

7. The state of Israel has existed since 1948.

8. Happiness is watching the Jewish army and knowing that the Spirit of Zion cannot live without a body and that this army is the guarantor of that body's existence.

9. The Palestinian birthright to our land is unquestionable.

10. The Jewish Awakening came simultaneously with the Arab Awakening.

11. Jerusalem is the eternal capital of Humankind.

12. Islam, alone of the three monotheistic faiths, embraces the other two in its ken.

13. PLO leader Yasser Arafat has openly indicated his willingness to recognize Israel within the framework of bilateral recognition.

14. One poll found that 31.8 percent of the Israeli's public regarded Jewish terrorist actions as either fully or partly justified.

15. Jewish destiny justifies the ousting of the Palestinians.

16. The Palestinian culture will never reach the sophistication of our Jewish heritage.

17. The territory known in modern times as the West Bank has been renamed with its biblical labels, Judea and Samaria.

# Bibliography

The following list of books, periodicals, and pamphlets deals with the subject matter of this chapter.

Bernard Avishai — *The Tragedy of Zionism: Revolution and Democracy in the Land of Israel*. New York: Farrar, Straus & Giroux, 1985.

Charles E. Brewster — "Islam and 'Barbaric Modernity,'" *The Christian Century*, November 6, 1985.

Simha Flapan — "Israelis and Palestinians: Can They Make Peace?" *Journal of Palestine Studies*, Autumn 1985.

David Ignatius — "The Middle East Is Everybody's Fault," *The Washington Monthly*, November 1984.

E.G.H. Joffe — "Arab Nationalism and Palestine," *Journal of Peace Research*, vol. 20, 1983.

Daoud Kuttab — "When Violence Begets Violence: Israel's Intransigence Fuels Palestinian Frustration," *Los Angeles Times*, October 11, 1985.

Nikolai Larichev — "A Strike Force of Imperialism," *Soviet Military Review*, October 11, 1985.

Flora Lewis — "Mideast Deadlines," *The New York Times*, October 29, 1985.

Conor Cruise O'Brien — "Why Israel Can't Take 'Bold Steps' for Peace," *The Atlantic Monthly*, October 1985.

Shimon Peres — "Excerpts from Speech Proposing Talks," *The New York Times*, October 22, 1985.

Yehoshua Porath — "Mrs. Peter's Palestine," *The New York Review of Books*, January 16, 1986.

Edward W. Said — *The Question of Palestine*. New York: Random House, 1979.

Hassan Bin Talal — "Return to Geneva," *Foreign Policy*, Winter 1984/85.

Lally Weymouth — "Israel's Dilemma," *The New Republic*, August 26, 1985.

Leon Wieseltier — "Kahane: The Making of a Jewish Monster," *The New Republic*, November 21, 1985.

# General Bibliography

The following list of books and periodicals deals with the subject matter of this book.

Robert Coles — *The Political Life of Children*. Boston, MA: The Atlantic Monthly Press, 1986.

Henry Steele Commager — "Of Virtue and Foreign Policy," *Worldview*, October 1982.

Leonard W. Doob — *Patriotism and Nationalism: Their Psychological Foundations*. Westport, CT: Greenwood Press, 1976.

Desmond Fennell — *Beyond Nationalism*. Swords, Ireland: Ward River Press, 1985.

Ernest Gellner — *Nations and Nationalism*. Ithaca, NY: Cornell University Press, 1983.

Hans Kohn — *The Age of Nationalism*. New York: Harper and Brothers, 1962.

Hans Kohn — "Nationalism: Is It Good or Bad?" *Foreign Policy Bulletin*, October 15, 1957.

Hans Kohn — *Nationalism: Its Meaning and History*. New York: Van Nostrand Reinhold Company, 1965.

Hans Morgenthau — "Paradoxes of Nationalism," *Yale Review*, June 1957.

R.A. Norem — "Is the Nation-State Obsolete?" *Christian Century*, October 6, 1937.

Charley Reese — "Liberals Apologize for Nationalism," *Manchester Union Leader*, August 14, 1984.

J.V. Schall — "Does a Bell Toll for the Nation-State?" *America*, August 7, 1971.

Helmut Schmidt — *The Anachronism of National Strategy: The Reality of Interdependence*. New Haven, CT: Yale University Press, 1986.

Dudley Seers — *The Political Economy of Nationalism*. New York: Oxford University Press, 1983.

Boyd C. Shafer — *Nationalism and Internationalism: Belonging in Human Experience*. Melbourne, FL: Krieger, 1982.

Barbara Ward — *Five Ideas That Change the World*. New York: W.W. Norton and Company, Inc., 1959.

# Index